KYŪDŌ
The Art of Zen Archery

Hans Joachim Stein was born in Germany in 1945. He studied History and Pedagogics at Hanover University, and now lives in Osaka in Japan where he is a Professor of International Cultural Studies. A Japanese speaker, he has practised Taoist and Buddhist meditation techniques for over 10 years and holds the grade of 3rd dan in Kyūdō.

K Y Ū D Ō
THE ART OF ZEN ARCHERY

Hans Joachim Stein

Translated by Frauke and Tim Nevill

ELEMENT BOOKS

© Hans Joachim Stein 1988

First English language edition published 1988 by
Element Books Ltd
Longmead, Shaftesbury, Dorset

Originally published as
Die Kunst des Bogen schiessens Kyūdō
by Scherz Verlag

Printed and bound by Billings, Hylton Road, Worcester
Typesetting by Poole Typesetting (Wessex) Ltd.,
Bournemouth BH1 2JN

Designed by Max Fairbrother

British Library Cataloguing in Publication Data
Stein, Hans Joachim
  Kyūdō : the art of Zen archery.
  1. Archery — Japan 2. Marital arts
  — Religious aspects — Zen Buddhism
  I. Title
  799.3'2   GV1188.J3

ISBN 1-85230-035-3

CONTENTS

Preface by Robert Schinzinger

Part I: Historical Foundations

Part II: The Spiritual Foundations of Kyūdō

Part III: The Practice of Kyūdō

●

Part IV: The Kyūdō Archer's Equipment

PREFACE

One of the unspoken premises of all ancient Japanese sports implies that whatever is physical is also spiritual, and that death stands at the very centre of life. Nietzsche said of the Greeks and Romans that their vital consciousness was different from ours because death had a different meaning for them. That also applies to Japan. Even though the bow is no longer a military weapon there, ancient ideas about life and death have been preserved in the art of archery. The knowledge is still alive that archery is not simply a form of physical exercise but a 'Way' (Jap. *dō*) of spiritual training and a philosophy which looks death in the eye.

It thus becomes clear that Kyūdō, the 'Way of the Bow', is a physico-spiritual discipline whose ultimate goal is the development and perfection of the person and personality of whosoever practises this art. The attainment manifested in the actions involved in shooting the bow, and the demonstration of the degree of spiritual maturity achieved, are as important as hitting the target. Practice of this art is intended to lead to deeper understanding of oneself and of the world by way of a discipline of body and mind. The principal methods are concentration and meditation, with correct breathing playing a crucial part. According to Japanese tradition, all practice should result in a higher level of maturity. The puny, egotistical lower self, which is caught up in appearances, has to be overcome in favour of the deeper true Self inherent in all human beings. To attain this spiritual attitude, the technique of Kyūdō has to be mastered as perfectly as possible. The spiritual and the technical elements become an organic unity through persistent, serious practice. That explains the close connection between Kyūdō and Zen Buddhism which developed on the soil of Chinese Taoism, reached a peak in the China of the Tang Dynasty, and arrived in Japan in the twelfth century. This book therefore also deals with the mutual interpenetration of Taoism and Zen, showing how this extremely fruitful synthesis finds concrete expression in the act of shooting an arrow. The spiritual background and the practical requirements of handling the bow are given equal emphasis, so

vii

PREFACE

this book is one of the first to provide well-founded assistance for the reader who intends to take up – or is already practising – Kyūdō, as well as for anyone who is more interested in gaining insight into its spiritual foundations.

The reader may ask whether the 'Way of the Bow', which is ultimately a path to self-knowledge, can still lay claim to importance within the rush of life in our highly industrialised society. In this connection it is worth noting that the essentials of archery – determination, persistence, and self-discipline – account in part for the great success of Japanese industry. At any rate, Hans Joachim Stein, who teaches at a Japanese University and holds the Third Dan in Kyūdō, is well qualified to answer the question more fully.

As I write these lines, the coldest time of the year is beginning in Japan. During the early hours of the day, young men and women carrying big bows are occasionally to be seen on their way to practise 'the discipline of the coldest time'.

Robert Schinzinger
Yokohama, New Year 1984

PART I

HISTORICAL FOUNDATIONS

HISTORICAL FOUNDATIONS

The Historical Significance of the Bow

The bow has existed almost everywhere in the world ever since the Palaeolithic Era – or at least since the Neolithic Age. It was used for hunting and in war, but arrows also served as 'fire-drills' for starting fire, and the sound peculiar to the bowstring may have been the primordial impulse for development of plucked or string instruments. Tasmania and Australia (except for a few limited areas in the north) are the only places where no indications of the bow's Stone Age use have been discovered so far. Exactly where the bow, mankind's oldest shooting weapon alongside the catapult, was first invented remains an unanswered question. Research to date suggests that there was probably no connection between its initial introduction in the Middle East, India, East Asia, Africa, and Europe. As a cultural achievement invention of the bow may well be compared to the domestication of fire.

From the dawn of mankind the bow's high effectiveness led to its association with magic and the gods. The fact that stone arrowheads produced sparks when they hit rock probably played a part in that. The earliest depictions of the use of bow and arrow date back to before the development of pottery – to *c.* 8,000–7,000 BC in the Middle East of the Neolithic Age. The famous cave paintings of eastern Spain with their magical depictions of hunting and war, and the well-known rock drawings in Sweden, are almost equally ancient. The first known depictions of the composite bow (constructed of several laminations of wood or other material such as horn – as opposed to the simple bow made from a single piece of wood) were produced in Mesopotamia in the 4th millennium BC. This type of bow, which surpassed the simple bow in strength and pliability, was common all over Asia, particularly in the Middle East, and probably spread from there into the Mediterranean area. It was also found among some of the Indian tribes of North America. The two ends of most composite bows point towards the target when such a bow is not drawn. That is why this type of bow is also called a reflex bow.

Palaeolithic wooden bows – unlike stone arrowheads – have only been preserved as visual depictions. The first original objects to survive the process of natural decay date back to the Mesolithic period (10,000–3,000 BC) in Northern Europe, to Swiss lake dwellings of the Neolithic period (3,000–1,800 BC), and to Egyptian tombs where from the First Dynasty (2,900–2,760 BC) onwards extremely elaborate bows were often buried with the dead.

The first record of bows being deployed on a large scale in a battle comes from the peoples of Akkad in the third millennium BC. Bowmen usually went into action at the beginning of a battle, during sieges, during combat on horseback, and in naval encounters where longer distances were involved. The bow was a devastating weapon of war, especially when it was deployed by lightly armed horsemen or warriors in fast-moving, extremely manoeuvrable chariots, exemplifying military skills particularly highly developed among the ancient peoples of the Middle East. A palace relief (c. 640 BC) from Nineveh, depicting scenes from the battle where Ashurbanipal finally defeated the Elamites, provides very striking testimony to the turbulent nature of such hostilities.

Among the nomadic peoples of the Middle East, the Scythians were probably the most successful in deploying the bow and arrow as their principal weapon. Around 513 King Cyrus tried to overcome, once and for all, the danger threatening Persia from that tribe of horsemen which originally came from the region north of the Black Sea. As is well known, he failed, and so did Darius a year later. The armies of Scythian horsemen proved to be superior to the Persians, especially in terms of speed and manoeuvrability, and their horse-archers inflicted terrible losses on their opponents. The Scythians ultimately advanced across the Dniepr into the Balkans, where they got as far as the Danube, the Pannonian Plain, and the area south of the Carpathian Mountains. Later they penetrated even further, reaching Bavaria and what became known as the Brandenburg Marches. They invaded Northern Italy too, together with the Thracians, who also enjoyed a high reputation as bowmen.

The Huns are a better-known instance of the striking power of nomadic armies of horsemen using the bow as their main weapon. With their recurrent raids in the second-century BC they long presented a serious threat to the Chinese Han Empire. Later their speedy horse-archers terrified the whole of Europe until, under Attila, they were finally defeated by Flavius Aetius in AD 451 on the Catalaunian Fields (near what is today Chalons-sur-Marne).

From the middle of the second millennium BC, the position of dominant great power was only attained by peoples which could deploy armies of bowmen who went into combat in chariots or on horseback. After the conquest of Asia by the Scythians, those armies of horsemen sprang up everywhere in the Middle East and soon began to dominate warfare there. Their tactics demanded the highest degree of skill in handling horses and weapons. Warriors on horseback had to keep their hands free even when galloping, and use of their principal weapon required just as much skill. They had to be accurate in hitting their target whilst riding at breakneck speed, often shooting their arrows backwards over one shoulder. Superior horsemanship in conjunction with unsurpassable skill in use of the bow were among the factors leading to both the rise of the great Asian empires and also the threat posed by Huns, Mongols, Arabs, and Turks to the very existence of the occidental empires. Only the invention of firearms put an end to the superiority of those armies of horse-archers.

'The bow, the long-range weapon characteristic of the vast steppes, was hated by both the Greeks with their agonic attitude to combat and the Germanic heroes,'[1] notes Heinz Meyer. The ideal of sportive context expressed in the word *agon* to a large extent determined the Greek view of combat, even in war. Similarly the Teutonic attitude to battle – namely that even though battle was a matter of life and death, it was primarily an honourable struggle between two heroes charged with defending or asserting their own or their tribe's repute – prevented European warriors from adequately assessing the bow's worth and from employing it effectively. In both cultures it was considered unfair, dishonourable, unmanly, and even cowardly to deliberately evade honourable hand-to-hand combat by resorting to the long-range bow, anonymously shooting arrows (possibly even from an ambush), and making use of a horse for a quick, often only feigned escape, and then suddenly attacking again, equally perfidiously in new formation and from a different direction. For the Greeks and Ancient Germans the bow thus only played a role in mythology – a very marginal one in the latter case.

5

Occasionally, mighty and invincible bows are mentioned in accounts of Viking sea-battles. The impressive Bayeux tapestry in Normandy (Bayeux, Musée de la Reine Mathilde), which depicts William the Conqueror's victory over the Anglo-Saxons at the battle of Hastings (1066) and the conquest of England, does, however, illustrate the Normans' deployment of the bow. Nevertheless sword and lance remained the undisputed primary and preferred weapons in Europe.

The bow and arrow never established themselves among the Romans either, even though the security of the Empire in its later stages was largely dependent on archers – foreign 'specialists' with oriental mercenaries or allies supplying the units whose main weapon was the bow.

European archery culminated in the English longbow made from yew, which measured as much as 1.90 m. and is only surpassed in length by the Japanese Kyūdō bow (approximately 2.10 m.). The English longbowmen were amazingly successful during the Hundred Years War (1339–1453) when England tried to impose its claim to the French throne. The dreaded longbow was predominantly used by freehold farmers known as yeomen. That was one of the main reasons why the war became a matter of national pride for the English people. The traditionalist French army of knights was often no match for this 'people's army' in which all social classes were represented. The English archers' well-founded pride in their achievements was partly responsible for prolonged and surprisingly stubborn resistance to the introduction of much more costly firearms which the yeoman could not anyway afford. Because of that tradition the bow continued to enjoy undiminished popularity in England, even when it had ceased to be of much value as a military weapon. The first English archery clubs were founded as early as the seventeenth century.

The last time the bow was employed as a weapon of war was by Polish cavalry units fighting against Napoleon in 1807.

Archery made its first appearance as an Olympic discipline during the 1900 Games at Paris. Competitions in St Louis (1904), London (1908), and Antwerp (1920) followed, but after that there was a break of fifty-two years before archery's return to the 1972 Olympic Games at Munich.

The record distance to date was achieved at Constantinople by Sultan Selim of Turkey in 1798. Turks had been enthusiastic and much-feared archers from time immemorial. The Sultan's arrow, shot from a Turkish reflex bow made from horn and the sinews of a bull's neck, covered the astounding distance of 972 yards and 2¾ inches (approximately 900 m.). The greatest range attained by a modern bow is around 700 m. Yamaha Gumbe from Japan reached 450 m. with his Kyūdō bow, establishing what is considered a record for that type of bow.

The History of the Bow in Japan

Japanese culture is of surprisingly recent origin compared with the great cultures of the Asian mainland and the Mediterranean area. Egyptian, Indian, Cretan, Semite, Greek, and Persian cultures extend back into far more ancient times. The comparison with China is especially striking and of considerable significance for this investigation. From their earliest beginnings Japanese history and culture have been intimately linked with those of the Asian mainland, and particularly with China. In all probability, Chinese culture itself enjoyed mutual contact with the cultures of Central Asia right from the start.

Chinese influences inclusive of traditions dating back to more ancient cultures reached the Japanese archipelago by way of Korea. It has justly been pointed out that Japanese culture presupposes that of the Chinese mainland – although too much is often made of that. Too much because that view, which is basically correct, may easily leave out of account the fact that the influences reaching Japan were not simply taken over and preserved, but were creatively integrated into the local culture and modified so as to benefit it. The chief impulses were, however, mainly Chinese in origin.

Japan's first inhabitants were ethnic groups with differing racial characteristics rather than being indigenous to the chain of islands. They had begun leaving the southern part of Central Asia around 30,000 BC, migrating eastwards, and finally reached (among other places) Japan, unable to travel further. In prehistoric times the Japanese chain of islands was still partly linked with the mainland, and where the land had been covered by the sea the water was shallow enough to make the crossing relatively easy. Later, however, the sea-bed sunk and the archipelago was largely cut off from the mainland. The proto-caucasian Ainu appear to have been the survivors of one of those

7

first migrant groups. There are still between 15,000 and 16,000 of those people on Hokkaido, an island in the northernmost part of Japan. They were later called Kumaso (from Jap. *kuma,* bear – an animal worshipped by the Ainu) or Ebisu (barbarians) – and the Japanese still despise them as such. The process of their displacement northwards and their total subjugation was only completed during the eighteenth century. Although the exact origins of the Ainu remain disputed up to the present day – some experts believe them to be of Malayan and others of Mongolian descent – yet others maintain that they are a mixture of the two – it is certain that this people used bows and arrows for their hunting. Their bow consisted of a short piece of wood (Simple Bow) with a string of animal-derived material. This bow – for which the Ainu also used poisoned arrows – did not spread over the whole chain of islands. It remained restricted to this ethnic group, so there is no link with the more recent bow of Japanese origin.

Another wave of migrants reached the Japanese archipelago at about the same time as the Ainu – though conclusive research evidence to date their arrival is simply not available. This new group is said to have been related to the forest cultures of North-East Asia. The question of their origin has not, however, been completely resolved either. This group later became bearers of the Jōmon culture (*c.* 10,000–250 BC), named after the characteristic cord-impressed decoration of its elaborate pottery, the earliest discovered on earth so far. Anthropologically neither the Ainu nor the representatives of the Jōmon culture had features corresponding to those of today's Japanese population, which is essentially of Mongolian descent. It is also still unknown whether the Jōmon culture itself invented the techniques used in producing pottery, imported the relevant knowledge from the Asian mainland, or only acquired it on the Japanese archipelago. Archaeological finds of more recent origin on the Asian mainland suggest that this great cultural achievement may well have originated there, and is not necessarily to be attributed to the Jōmon population of Japan. Japanese archeologists now accept that future excavations in Korea will probably bring to light objects similar to the Jōmon discoveries.

The same is true of the Jōmon bow. Even though it was only developed shortly after the invention of pottery – at least no more ancient finds have been excavated so far – the immigrants may have brought knowledge of the bow with them too. At any rate, arrowheads made of flint (like those of the Jōmon people) have also been discovered on the Asian mainland. The most ancient bows preserved in Japan were found on the Torihama site in the Fukui prefecture. The find in question consisted of two bows which date back to the ancient Jōmon culture and were probably made between 7,000 and 6,000 BC. One of them measures 1.29 m. the other exactly 1 m. Surprisingly, these bows made of Kaya wood (*Torreya nucifera*) were even at that early date bound from top to bottom with strips of birch, probably in order to increase the bow's strength and suppleness, and thus prevent it from breaking too quickly – an amazing technique considering that extensive binding is really the characteristic of the composite bow whose different layers of material were thereby held together more securely. It is, however, also possible that the binding material wrapped around the Jōmon bows reflects the artistic sensibility of those people, since the string patterns of their pottery bear a striking resemblance to the bindings on their bows.

Several bows dating back to the New Jōmon Period (from around 1,000 BC) have also been excavated – some preserved whole, others only in part. Like the oldest Jōmon bows, these too consist of a simple wooden stave and vary in length from 70 cm. to 2 m. Astonishingly, some of these bows were lacquered, most probably in order to make them weatherproof. The differing lengths of the bows are not likely to be of special significance, and are probably to be explained simply by the lengths of wood available. This was only cut if its length considerably exceeded that of the archer's height when a bow would become unwieldly. The materials most frequently employed were the branches of the Matsu (pine), Kaya, or Kuwa (the mulberry tree whose leaves furnish the silkworm with food). It is certain that the early Jōmon bows were not composite but simple bows fashioned from a single piece of wood. Descriptions that maintain the contrary contradict all recent Japanese archaeological reports, which do not mention any laminated composite or reflex bows in connection with either the Jōmon period or the subsequent Yayoi epoch.[2]

In about the third century AD a further wave of immigrants, consisting of groups of Mongolians, arrived from Southern China and Korea. Larger ethnic groups were driven out of those areas by wars and expansion of the Chinese Empire under the Ch'in Dynasty (221–207 BC) which united China for the first time. The successor Han Dynasty (206 BC – AD 220) pursued such expulsions. Those groups clearly belonged to a Mongolian race. Once they had reached the Japanese archipelago they established the Yayoi culture there after having interbred – albeit probably to a very limited extent – with people from the Jōmon culture. According to modern research, today's Japanese are their descendants. Earlier assumptions linking them with the Jōmon or Ainu are now thought generally incorrect.

The Jōmon and the Yayoi are clearly of different origins, both racially (the Jōmon people are not of Mongolian descent) and in terms of their artefacts. The pottery of the Yayoi culture, named after the site where its first artefacts were discovered, is more sparsely decorated than that of the Jōmon culture. The Yayoi people already possessed the pottery wheel, and knew how to smelt iron and produce bronze. They already pursued agriculture, and had brought with them from the mainland horses, cows, and paddy-cultivation of rice. In later settlements numerous objects from the Chinese Han Dynasty were found – including coins, mirrors, and bronze bells, as well as such weapons as spears and swords. All in all, the arrival of this ethnic group or groups entailed a completely new technological order for the islands of Japan – as compared with the Jōmon culture of gathering and hunting. Despite the partial interpenetration of the two cultures, resulting in regional modifications of the Yayoi culture which gradually came to predominate, the Jōmon culture finally completely disappeared. It obviously did not add any essential element to the way of life of the Japan to come – unlike the Yayoi culture.

While the Jōmon people were still making their arrowheads from stone, the Yayoi were already able to forge iron tips. If they originally made frequent use of flint tips and continued to do so occasionally, that was because the production of flint arrowheads was simpler and less time-consuming. Spent arrows often could not be found again and had to be replaced quickly. The demand for arrows must have been considerable since the start of rice cultivation brought about conflicts over land and water rights.

The most ancient artistic depiction of bow and arrow found up to now also dates back to the Yayoi Period. This is the decoration on a bronze bell (third century BC) depicting hunting scenes and showing (among other things) an archer who has just shot an arrow. The archer is holding his bow about two-thirds down its total length. The Yayoi bow was thus clearly asymmetrical like today's Kyūdō bow. The reason for this asymmetry, which the Jōmon bow did not have, is probably to be found in the hunting techniques of the early Yayoi. When fishing, they held the bow steadily just above the surface of the water and waited until a fish had come close enough. Bows with shorter lower limbs were naturally more suitable for this purpose.

This patient waiting, which even today is a characteristic especially cultivated by the Japanese, also seems to have been practised during hunting on land and in situations of armed conflict. That appears to be confirmed by a number of skulls with holes in the cranium dating back to the Yayoi Period. Apparently the attacker must have crouched in a tree whilst awaiting his adversary's arrival, and then shot him from above. Such behaviour, demanding that the weapon be held at the ready for a considerable time, is facilitated by a bow with a shorter lower section. Were the bow only to be lifted once the victim or prey had come within comfortable range, that movement would have revealed the bowman or scared off the prey.

Because of its asymmetry, the Yayoi bow can in all probability be regarded as the prototype of the Japanese Kyūdō bow. To the best of my knowledge, that form has remained unique on earth to this day. The asymmetrical shape was retained even when a length of around 2 m. later became the norm for bows since it considerably facilitated their handling, particularly when shooting from horseback (Jap. *yabusame*). The oldest Yayoi finds from a site at Nabatake in Saga province included four bows, each averaging about 80 cm. in length and made from a single piece of wood.

All subsequent epochs in Japan, from the Yamato Period (300–710 AD) to the Heian Period (794–1192 AD) only knew the simple bow made from a single stave. During the Heian Period, around the beginning of the eleventh century, the first composite bows, known as Fuse-dake-yumi (*fuse*, to cover; *take*, bamboo; *yumi*, bow) started to appear. To begin with, only their outer layer consisted of bamboo. The traditional round wooden bow also continued in use, however, since the new bows were easily broken because of imperfect manufacturing techniques, and the material around the bow did not hold it together sufficiently.

Ultimately bows were produced with up to four laminations of bamboo. They gradually completely supplanted the old round timber bow because of their increased sturdiness and improved efficiency. This development in bow construction seems only to have been concluded at the time of the Gempei War (1180–1185), fought between rival families in the Taira and Minamoto clans, and during the following Kamakura Period (1185–1333). The

11

Heian period was distinguished by – among other things – active contacts with its powerful Chinese neighbour, which had already long been in possesion of the composite bow. There is every reason to believe that it was at this time that the composite bow reached Japan from China together with other cultural artefacts.

Archery was essentially practised as Kyū-jutsu until well into the Kamakura Period. The technical elements of archery predominated although the formal and spiritual aspects were not unknown. Confucianism, which recommended archery as a means of perfecting the personality (albeit from a more formal point of view), had, after all, become established in Japan as early as the fourth century. At the end of the twelfth and the beginning of the thirteenth century, Zen Buddhism was brought to Japan by the Zen monk Eisai (1141–1215). When Zen came into close contact with the Kamakura Shōgunate, the martial arts of Japanese warriors (Samurai, Bushi) also began to change. The concept of Kyū-jutsu continued to exist until well into the Tokugawa period (1600–1868), but Zen Buddhist ideas were adopted by the Samurai at an early date. These directed the warrior's thoughts away from the issue of life *or* death, and instead made him contemplate them as an inseparable unity, as the two poles of one whole which belong together and complement one another. The mind's release from the problems of life and death, victory and defeat, made possible highly effective, undivided concentration on the act of combat itself. Already during the Kamakura period many Samurai began to assimilate the disciplines of Zen Buddhism in the context of their instruction and training – sometimes under the instigation of their leaders. This training proved its worth during the two invasions by Mongols in 1274 and 1281, especially during the latter when the Samurai achieved considerable successes against the numerically superior Mongol forces. Both invasions were, however, ultimately beaten back by 'Heaven-sent' typhoons, the Kamikaze (the 'Godly Winds'), which sunk most of the Mongol ships.

After shipwrecked Portuguese introduced matchlock muskets to Japan in 1543, archery became all-embracingly the 'Way of the Bow', a way to the archer's own Self and to union with the universe and its energies. As early as 1575, Oda Nobunaga, commanding an army equipped with muskets, defeated a larger force of Samurai cavalry traditionally armed with sword and bow at Nagashino. Ironically, however, Oda Nobunaga was later fatally wounded by an arrow and set fire to the Honnoji temple in

Kyōto where he had entrenched himelf during another conflict, before committing traditional *seppuku* (suicide by disembowelment).

The concept of *dō* ('Way'; Chin. *Tao*) had, however, already long permeated Kyū-jutsu, the art and technique of archery, and in 1660 Morikawa Kosan, a master of archery, coined the term Kyūdō (*kyū*, bow; *dō*, way). Despite the progress of firearms, the Way of the Bow was continually cultivated by monks as a means of meditation and by the aristocracy as a sport – but even in the latter case not infrequently as an aid on the way towards self-knowledge and overcoming the 'little I'. Since mythological times the bow has also been, and still is being, used in conjunction with countless ceremonies and traditional customs.

The bow remained almost exclusively in the hands of the aristocracy until in 1868 Japan was virtually forced by the USA to open its doors to the West. In the year of Japan's enforced opening up and the reinstatement of the Tennō (the Japanese Emperor whose office had been administered by the Shōguns ever since the Kamakura era's military regime), Emperor Meiji's government proposed the total abolition of all forms of traditional martial arts such as Jūdō, Karate, Kendō, and Kyūdō because they were said to belong to the past. That measure did not, however, have the desired effect. It must be seen in the broader context of endeavours to open up Japan to Western ideas as far as possible, adapting it to Western culture even to the extent of trying to throw overboard traditions deeply rooted in the Japanese character.

The warrior class, the main pillar of society up to the end of the Tokugawa period, was dissolved, and the Samurai were either raised to the nobility or incorporated in the middle class. To the horror of the Samurai, compulsory military service was introduced in 1871. They thereby lost their privileges and had to witness helplessly how *every* male Japanese citizen, regardless of class, could be called up for such service. In 1876 the Samurai were even forbidden to carry swords. Traditionally there existed a close connection between the classical martial arts such as Kyūdō and Kendō (*ken*, sword; *dō*, way) and the warrior class, so the latter also became caught up in democratisation to such an extent that it finally had to renounce the iemoto system (*ie*, house, family; *moto*, root).

All the other traditional arts such as the Japanese tea ceremony, flower arranging, etc., have retained that system. The iemoto stands at the head of each art, and every disciple, from the lowest to the highest, is linked with the iemoto through a hierarchical system of master–pupil relationships. That guarantees success to the pupil and enormous profits to the higher teaching ranks – especially to the iemoto himself. For a Westerner a diploma costs an incredible sum. Apart from the tuition fees, which are high enough, every teacher can count on considerable gifts at particular times of the year, often in the form of money. Most of this goes into the pockets of the iemoto and his closest subordinates. The higher the rank, the more substantial the sum of money passed upwards. The pupil–teacher relationship cannot ever be dissolved either, let alone reversed, even if the pupil should eventually prove to be superior to his teacher.

The abolition of the iemoto system in the martial arts, which was finally completed when the traditional martial arts were temporarily prohibited during the American occupation at the end of World War II, resulted in the surprising paradox that to this very day the classic Samurai preoccupations come closest to Western ideas about organisational democracy and relative openness towards the outside world. Anybody who is interested can take up the Way of Kyūdō, regardless of their financial situation. In the martial arts one only has to reckon with normal membership fees, whereas in other traditional arts each pupil is subjected to enormous financial burdens.[3]

In 1945 the American occupying power prohibited Kyūdō and other Budō disciplines because they were thought to contribute towards resurgence of the military spirit. The Americans may have thereby brought about relative democratisation within the martial arts, but that prohibition strengthened and intensified interest in those very arts, making them even more popular than they already were. The All-Japanese Kyūdō Association (*Zen Nippon Kyūdō Remmei*) was established as early as 1948, and today has a membership of around 600,000 archers.

The meditative aspects of Kyūdō have largely survived to this day, but renewed emphasis on technical aspects is also undeniable. The many competitions and championships held every year, attracting thousands of spectators, contribute towards that. These include the All-Japanese Championships, national sports festivals, competitions amongst prefectures and municipal districts, events at the Imperial Palace in which only the best archers from the prefectures are allowed to take part, and contests among today's Kyūdō schools (*Heki-ryū*, *Honda-ryū*, and *Ogasawara-ryū: ryū* – school, doctrine) which have mostly been won up to now by the *Heki-ryū* archers, as well as championships and competitions exclusively for high-school pupils, students, and employees and workers. Nearly every larger university has a Kyūdō club. From time to time television transmits Kyūdō demonstrations and reports on competitions. Some of the bigger firms even have their own Kyūdō halls where employees can practise several times a week – after their work is done.

PART II

THE SPIRITUAL
FOUNDATIONS
OF KYŪDŌ

THE SPIRITUAL FOUNDATIONS
OF KYŪDŌ

Breath and Breathing

'In Kyūdō correct breathing is as important as bow and arrow themselves. Without correct breathing, no satisfactory shot.'

Many masters begin any practical instruction with that basic advice. In fact, anyone who has ever picked up a bow and shot an arrow towards a target will have felt and known instantly if his breathing was wrong. That shot will have been the outcome of strained effort.

Such coarse violence makes one feel sorry for bow and arrow, and also for the archer because an observer can see that the bowman is left with a very unpleasant feeling of disharmony. Dissatisfaction with himself starts the moment he has released the arrow, seeing it whirr unsteadily towards the target which will at best be hit by chance.

Those feelings of dissatisfaction with oneself, unhappiness about the action just performed, and inner disharmony resulting from wrong and unnatural breathing are not restricted to archery. In all situations in life, inadequate breathing leads to lack of balance accompanied by tension, and is often the reason for organic bodily disorders – and not just in extreme cases.

It may be helpful here to consider the function and significance of breath and breathing for both body and mind.[1] The origins of the ideas underlying all the traditional martial arts of China and Japan will be examined before more detailed attention is devoted to the part breathing plays in Kyūdō. Most people know about the importance of breathing for body and mind but few are really aware of its true significance, and even fewer employ a simple and undemanding breathing technique in their everyday existence.

From a biological and medical point of view, air has to be seen as essentially our main 'food', our 'daily bread' in terms of both quality and quantity, because the human body is constituted of 65 per cent oxygen, 18 per cent carbon dioxide, and 10 per cent hydrogen. Hence air makes up 93 per cent of our bodily existence. That explains why the different yogic schools and the meditative disciplines of Tantrism, Buddhism, and Taoism lay such stress on correct breathing as one of the preconditions for healthy living and one of the means towards spiritual growth and self-knowledge.

Inadequate, unnatural, and shallow breathing have a negative effect on the whole breathing apparatus: the throat, bronchial tubes, thorax, abdomen, and diaphragm. Waste products and gaseous residues accumulate in ever greater quantities and poison the whole body slowly but surely. In conjunction with insufficiency of oxygen supply and distribution, that leads to indigestion, over-sensitivity, anxiety feelings, disturbed sleep, insomnia, and numerous other complaints. In extreme cases, there may result heart attacks, cardiac infarction, and mental disorders. It stands to reason that such deficient breathing makes impossible any peak intellectual or physical achievement since concentration over any long period becomes sheer torment. Even concentration for short periods then demands unnatural effort, and many people resort to dangerous crutches by helping matters along with various chemical products, drugs, nicotine, or alcohol. The path towards creativity, serenity, and inner security remains hopelessly barred. The familiar attempt at 'pulling oneself together' only causes more tension, amounting to little more than self-deception which leads nowhere or, at most, to a dead end since the roots of the matter remain untouched.

Correct breathing, on the other hand, cleanses and purifies the body; protects it against illness; brings peace, security, and energy; and guarantees that the supply and distribution of oxygen are adequate for every specific situation and activity. Some Yoga schools and 'alchemical' and popular Taoism stress that man can both optimise his mental and physical capacities in every imaginable way and also rejuvenate himself and prolong his lifespan by a considerable number of years. Taoists later extended that notion to the conviction that one's own body can be used for the distillation of a kind of elixir of life by employing certain breathing methods in conjunction with other techniques including a variety of meditative sexual practices.

Yoga, Taoism, and Zen Buddhism agree that we do not only

take in air when we breathe. We also supply our body with something far more important. When man inhales, he absorbs a certain amount of the sum total of all the energies in the cosmos, a fraction of those energies upon which the very existence of life depends. Ultimately the entire universe consists of cosmic 'air' or energy, which Indians call *prana*, Chinese *ch'i*, and Japanese *ki*.

Matter in its various manifestations (including man) comes into being solely as a result of the processes within this cosmic energy, so that we can see every kind of life simply as a concentration of organised energy.

Through the breathing process we take in fundamental elements of the universe, use them for our physical and mental life-process, and then release them again. This bodily functioning entails immeasurable and inexhaustible possibilities. This very simple physical activity is not just the precondition for all life. It also provides the key to conscious access to the very sources of life itself, depending on whether and how man makes use of that. If man wants to avail himself of that truly golden key, he first needs to become as aware as possible of the fact that through breathing he enters into a kind of direct – and not merely mental – contact with the universe and all its boundless, life-giving energies. With that he has taken the first step into his own inner space, the first step on the way to his own centre – a way which certainly has its difficulties but is all the more rewarding for that.

Alan Watts expressed that very well from a different perspective: 'The individual is an "opening" through which the entire energy of the universe becomes conscious of itself – a whirlpool of vibrations through which it manifests itself as man, animal, flower, or star'.[2] Such thoughts are not new. They are to be found expressed with striking clarity in Indian religions, in Taoism, and in other earlier Chinese philosophical systems. It is therefore completely justifiable to say that man's crucial existential endeavours at that time – as long as 5,000 years ago in the case of China – were directed towards establishment of immediate contact with the elemental life of the cosmos.

Taoism has already been mentioned a number of times, and some Kyūdō-ka (bowmen) might object that although it is generally agreed that Zen Buddhism is to some extent related to Japanese archery, Taoism and its offshoots are not. Indeed, most Japanese are not at all aware of the influence Taoism has exerted, and continues to exert, on their culture because for centuries their social and political ethics have put emphasis on Confucian rules

21

and ideals. It may not be possible to establish any direct Taoist influences on today's Kyūdō, comprehended as the Way of the Bow, but John Blofeld says that Taoists in China until recently also practised archery as a method on the path towards Enlightenment, and undoubtedly used to employ it to that end in ancient times.[3] Zen was, however, essentially formed in China where it – even more than Buddhism previously – entered upon a symbiosis with Taoism and ideas that had remained vital across the centuries.

The theories concerning breath and breathing make that particularly clear because the breathing techniques of Zen Buddhism are based on Chinese Universism, which includes Taoism, and are inconceivable without that background. Indian yoga may also have involved similar theories and breathing practices, but it is generally accepted today that the old Chinese system developed earlier, or at least independently of yogic influences. Zen also only incorporated aspects of the breathing techniques taken over into a comprehensive system of its own. It employs those techniques primarily as the practical basis for its meditation as such, i.e. for the achievement of a particular state of mental and bodily poise which is an essential precondition for any kind of meditative contemplation.

As is well known, the roots of Buddhism are to be found in India and the Upanishads. Buddhism reached China in the course of the first century AD during the Han Period (221 BC – AD 220). Only during the sixth century AD was it followed by Zen Buddhism which had developed later when Bodhidharma – who was revered as the 28th patriarch in the Indian lineage and simultaneously as the 1st patriarch of Zen in China – came to that country. The development of Zen in India (Sanskrit: *dhyāna)* is often seen as the outcome of attempts at reform of what had become a degenerate form of the original Buddhism there. It may appear surprising that Buddhism could establish itself so quickly and relatively easily in China, a country looking back over millennia of cultural history. That becomes understandable, however, in view of the fact that Buddhism reached China in its universal and syncretic form of Mahāyāna, which was open to any stimulating influences. China was also experiencing a period of upheavals at that time, and general uncertainty prevailed everywhere. The North in particular was suffering from almost chaotic conditions. Confucianism had failed in its social and political aspects, and was obviously in decline. Chinese society was therefore open to any fresh idea which seemed sufficiently vital to overcome the crisis.

Despite all its efforts, Confucianism – a comparatively dry and wooden philosophy which had finally become ossified in formalities and conventions – had also never succeeded in effectively suppressing the old Taoist ideas among the population in general and intellectual circles in particular. That was not really surprising since both directions had sprung from the same roots, the ancient Universism and the principles of Yin and Yang (Jap. *in-yō*).

Those facts explain the astonishing readiness with which Buddhism – which in many respects resembled Taoism – and its later expression through Zen were adopted in China. Taoist principles were often employed in order to elucidate Buddhist teachings and their concept of Enlightenment. Tao-sheng (360–434 AD), one of the great pioneers of Buddhism and Zen in China, used this method particularly extensively.

The Buddha himself had originally been influenced by Yoga but substantially reduced the many complicated Yoga practices and difficult breathing techniques. That entailed both renunciation of the development of spectacular 'supernatural' powers and opened the way to Enlightenment for many more people. The fact that the Buddha rejected Yoga's excessive philosophical speculations, the over-emphasis on rites that had long become obscure, and not least yogic notions about God and gods was of ongoing importance with regard to dissemination of the new teaching in China. Although in the final analysis Buddhism and Yoga, despite all the metaphysical differences, aspire to the same goal, the systems of the two schools point in different directions. Indian elements play only a very peripheral part in the breathing techniques of Kyūdō, and Yoga can be left out of account in that respect.

One important difference between Taoists and orthodox Buddhists lies in the fact that many of the latter believe that the origin of all suffering is to be found in the transience, inconstancy, and eternal change found in all life, which ultimately amounts to total insecurity. Taoism and Zen, on the other hand, unconditionally acknowledge inconstancy and change *per se* as given fundamental components of existence. For them constancy is solely to be found in change itself. There is nothing negative in the perishing and death of what exists since dying signifies nothing but transformation which nobody can escape. It is therefore the aim of Taoists and Zen Buddhists alike to integrate themselves in the eternal cycle of change without resistance or senseless attempts at escape. Undreamt-of creativity is inherent in dying and inconstancy because they form the basis of every new life, every new beginning.

The West is also familiar with that idea. As Goethe wrote:

> Never prompted to that quest:
> Die and dare rebirth
> You remain a dreary guest
> On our gloomy earth.[4]

Once we have grasped and really experienced that, any fear will fall away from us and no false hope can ensnare us any longer. We will realise that death is the most creative factor in life, lacking the least element of suffering.

Meditative breathing is an excellent aid on the path to self-knowledge, to experience of the interdependence of individual and cosmos, and to realisation of the individual self in the given cosmic context. In other words, meditative breathing transforms our mind and enables man to rediscover his buried inner self. He thereby becomes conscious of the fact that he is an integral part of the universe, that the universe ultimately exists through him and he exists through the universe, and that the individual and the cosmos form an inseparable unity in the timeless alternation of coming into being and passing away. Happiness depends on living in the greatest possible degree of harmony with the universe and its energies and laws.

When a human being stops breathing, he or she also ends their present form of existence. Breathing and breath are the prerequisites for life. The West has also known since time immemorial about this central role of breathing, expressing that knowledge in such terms as 'breath of life'. That idea has, however, never expanded into an all-embracing philosophical system or been integrated into such a system. In Taoism and the meditative schools of Buddhism, on the other hand, the regulation of breath plays a significant part.

The central concept of Taoism is the Tao (Sino-Jap. *dō;* Jap. *michi)* meaning the cyclic movement and way of the universe, harmonious change in nature, and the creative principle of life. The Tao generates and sustains all things spontaneously out of itself, making them flower and perish. It is the eternally creative way and primordial ground, containing the beginning and end of all existence. Everything that is springs from the Tao and returns to the Tao. It is the Absolute, Pure Being, which, even though itself without beginning, nevertheless contains, as the beginning of all existence, everything in its potential state.[5] Tao is therefore of two kinds: Being and Non-Being. Hamlet's words 'To be or not to be' miss the essence of that view because Being and Non-Being form a whole that excludes any question of Being *or* Non-Being. Man can experience the Tao as Being because as Non-Being it already contains within itself all existence. Man has been given the inestimable possibility of becoming one, here and now in this life, with the way of the universe, with harmonious transformation within nature, and with the primordial creative principle itself. As transcendent Tao, as Non-Being, it is beyond our powers of comprehension. We may at best have a vague idea about it, but it remains hidden in darkness.

From the Tao spring the two complementary forces of Yin and Yang. Yin characterises the dark, deep (Earth), passive, generative female principle, while Yang represents the light, high (Sky), active, creative male principle. The regular succession of nature's seasons, of human birth and death, and of all growth, flowering, and perishing are dependent on creative interaction between those two principles expressing the laws of the Tao. The passive Yin carries all beings, the active Yang embraces them. United in breathing they constitute the Tao. There is a Tao of the universe and also a Tao of man. Man owes his life and his life-force to the union of Yin and Yang. He is a product of both since he consists of the same elements as the world and the universe. In the words of Lao-tzu, who probably lived in the fourth century BC and is regarded as the source of what is known as philosophical Taoism: Heaven's path is the Tao, which pervades, is contained in, and underlies everything.[6]

Another central Taoist notion – and also of importance in Kyūdō – is *wu-wei*, which signifies Non-Doing or 'Without Doing'. This concept was derived from contemplation of the universe and of nature, where everything happens without passion, without particular effort, calmly, naturally, and without any premeditation. The bud opens spontaneously without struggle; the overripe melon bursts open without perceptible volition. That is how man should act too, spontaneously and without self-consciousness. Lao-tzu says that man should practise 'Work without Doing' and imitate the Tao since the Tao is eternally without doing, even though there is nothing that was not created by it.[7]

The *wu-wei* principle has been misunderstood by many people who have only dipped into Taoist thinking, mistakenly interpreting this principle as an invitation to sluggish passivity or *laissez-faire*. *Wu-wei* signifies pure action, an extremely active stillness, and a spontaneity in activity which is not hampered by busy restlessness, action for action's sake, or the frantic desires of our little ego. *Wu-wei* means action in non-action, spontaneously doing exactly the right thing at exactly the right moment. That only becomes possible if there is active mindfulness. This completely natural, unintentional, quiet intentness, which – wanting nothing for itself – is always ready to do what is necessary, would, however, be obstructed by any outer desires. The Tao could then not flow through our essential nature, our thinking and action, could not develop within ourselves, and we would continually be bogged down in superficial activities.

Through *ch'i* (breath) we can achieve a harmonious balance between Yin and Yang within ourselves. This process of harmonisation is fundamental to any self-knowledge and self-realisation, to returning home to the Tao. We have already seen that our respiratory function puts us into direct contact with the universe and the sources of life. When we control our breathing, we attain a state of active stillness – inwardly and outwardly, mentally and physically – which corresponds to the *wu-wei* and balances the interplay of the passive Yin and the active Yang forces that determine our being. Those forces are brought into an optimal relationship to each other, bringing about stabilisation of body and mind. Without that fundamental poise no shot in Kyūdō will ever be satisfactory.

From that level of absolute and wide-awake stillness, the human being looks into his inner Self, becomes one with it, and can make peace with himself and the world around. To do that he need not suppress anything, not even his own I, as is so often wrongly assumed. He does not do anything except observe his true Self and his I. In that way he comes to know himself, and at the same time the nature of the world around him reveals itself to him of its own accord. The archer who practises with such an attitude acts without doing. He makes the necessary movements without conscious volition; he acts from inside without strain or effort. He and the bow with its specific demands are a single, purposeless, natural unity. If a person continues unswervingly on this path, he will gradually learn to integrate his life into the all-embracing rhythm of the cosmos. He will learn to balance his passions and to live in the Tao without having to struggle with himself or his environment since as Lao-tzu proclaims, nobody can quarrel with a man who does not quarrel. He is calm and serene, but full of creative energy.

The point of departure for that is regulation of the breath, which is most effectively achieved through meditation. There seems to be no other method whereby we can adjust our relationship to microcosmos and macrocosmos, becoming an integral part of the universe. Philosophical thought may be of help in returning to the roots of existence, but only on a purely philosophical and mental level. All purely philosophical endeavours are restricted to an essentially intellectual level and fail to attain the profundity of spiritual *and* material penetration which can be achieved by way of meditative breathing. Through meditation and breath control we can reach direct awareness of our union with nature and with the entire universe. In that way we are reborn. The previous artificial separation between subject and object will be overcome within ourselves, and they merge into one.

Meditation in this sense does not only mean the traditional sitting in a special posture. Meditation can be practised in any situation, and it is of no account whatsoever whether the body is at rest or active. Any action, such as archery, which proceeds from our centre can be just as meditative as sitting quietly. Any everyday action becomes a kind of creative meditation when we control our breathing, and with it body and mind.

An ancient maxim of Chinese Universism, of particular application to Taoism, says that stillness leads to Enlightenment. Stillness is attained by meditative breathing, but does not necessarily involve sitting quietly. Instead it entails a silence which comes from our innermost being, bringing forth and inspiring all our actions, even those which seem to be most insignificant. That is based on a very tangible practice of a non-mental nature. Through the purification of *ching*, breath is transformed; through the purification of breath, *shen* is transformed.[8] In its material form *ching* is sperm which provides the body with vitality, but it is also a cosmic force which we take in, use, and release again in the act of breathing. *Shen* also has to be viewed from two aspects. In connection with thinking, perception, feeling etc., it stands for ordinary consciousness. In its other aspect it is that primal spiritual consciousness which exists even before we are born only then to be submerged, but which can

27

be recovered through the previously described meditation.

Breath and breathing (*ch'i;* Jap. *ki*) are intimately related to the micro- and macrocosmos. According to Taoism, when *ch'i* condenses in space, something undivided, the One, comes into being. If that is then divided, Yin and Yang arise, the pair of opposites which govern the world. Meditative breathing harmonises Yin and Yang, and as a result man, the microcosmos which already contains the macrocosmos within itself, can uncover his Self, his original consciousness *shen*, and guard it against all negative outer influences. He thus achieves perfectly natural integration in the macrocosmos.

The Taoist system is totally geared to the practical aspects of self-realisation. In complete contrast to Western philosophies, no purely intellectual endeavour is involved. In Zen this practical component is even more apparent than in Taoism. As we shall see later, that made it possible for Zen to exert such fundamental influence on Japanese culture. Lao-tzu describes the connection between stillness and Enlightenment as follows:

> Empty yourself of everything.
> Let the mind rest at peace.
> The ten thousand things rise and fall
> while the Self watches their return.
>
> They grow and flourish, and then return to the source.
> Returning to the source is stillness, which is the way of nature.
> The way of nature is unchanging.
> Knowing constancy is insight.[9]

As a means of attaining the Tao, Lao-tzu also recommends the meditative breathing practices which had been known and employed long before his time:

> Carrying body and soul and embracing the one,
> Can you avoid separation?
> Attending fully and becoming supple,
> Can you be as a new-born babe?[10]

Anyone who regulates and concentrates his breathing, the 'Breath of Life' or cosmic energy, can achieve a balancing of soul and mind, a harmonisation of Yin and Yang. He can become like a little child, returning to his source.

In the 6th chapter of the Tao-te-ching, which is attributed to

Lao-tzu, de Groot even detects some direct reference to the fundamental role of meditative breathing:

'Feeding the soul so that one does not die is [acquisition of] the mysterious [celestial breath] and the female [terrestrial breath]. And the openings [the mouth and nose], through which these mysterious and female breaths enter, are the root and the base of the celestial and terrestrial influences [which exist in man]. They ought to be inhaled smoothly and slowly, as if they were to be preserved [in the body]. In using those breaths, no exertion is to be made'.[11]

That chapter is particularly obscure and has consequently given rise to the most diverse of interpretations, most of which seem plausible. John Blofeld and others legitimately see that chapter in connection with the meditative sexual practices of Taoism.[12] Chuang-tzu (second half of the fourth century BC), the most important of Lao-tzu's pupils, talks in his 6th and 15th chapters about some technical aspects of breathing:

The True Man of ancient times slept without dreaming and woke without care; he ate without savouring and his breath came from deep inside. The True Man breathes with his heels; the mass of men breathe with their throats. Crushed and bound down, they gasp out their words as though they were retching.[13]

This breathing 'from deep inside' (literally 'with his heels') points to the technique of abdominal respiration which is an absolutely indispensable prerequisite in all Zen arts and sports.

Exhaling and inhaling, getting rid of the old and assimilating the new, stretching like a bear and craning like a bird, this is but valetudinarianism, affected by professors of hygiene and those who try to preserve the body to the age of P'eng Tsu.[14]

P'eng Tsu is proverbial for great age, supposedly having lived for over 800 years. In this section Chuang-tzu also warns against overdoing things by wanting to bring about Enlightenment forcibly, but the bodily posture during exhalation and inhalation described here is particularly informative. 'Stretching like a bear and craning like a bird' provides a precise description of the physical posture and mental attitude one has to adopt in Kyūdō just before the arrow is released.

Without correct posture, correct and natural breathing is impossible. Without correct breathing, in turn, meditation is impossible, and often becomes physical and mental torment. Breath, or rather the cosmic energy taken in through respiration, cannot flow or be directed freely through the body – and the outcome is physical and mental tension. Since man is subject to the laws of gravity, he has to adapt his bodily activities accordingly. In Taoist meditation and Zen Buddhism's Za-zen the meditator has to sit in such a way that his nose and navel are in a straight line absolutely perpendicular to the floor. His backbone and neck are thus naturally vertical too.

In archery (as will be demonstrated in greater detail in the chapter on practical training) that basic posture is essentially maintained in all movements from the start until the shot is released – with the apparent exception that from the end of the *yugamae* stage to the release of the arrow *(hanare)* the head is turned left towards the target. 'Apparent' because, despite that rotation, neck and head must remain perfectly vertical on the torso while the nose is on a perpendicular parallel to navel, neck, and spine. Chuang-tzu's 'stretching like a bear' corresponds to the idea in Kyūdō that just before the shot the archer should have the feeling of pushing his head into the sky while his legs are deeply rooted in the earth. The arms, chest, and shoulders meanwhile 'crane like a bird' horizontal to the ground, the left side pointing towards the target, the right in the opposite direction.

In Kyūdō the whole body is breathing – that is to say, the energy absorbed through respiration is conducted into all the different parts of the body, including those which in the Za-zen sitting meditation are scarcely employed – particularly the legs. Chuang-tzu's instruction that one should 'breathe with one's heels' has no equivalent in Za-zen. Otherwise everything that has been said about Taoist breathing in this chapter also applies in principle to breathing in Zen meditation. After all, as we have already seen, as far as its theory and practices are concerned Zen Buddhism essentially goes back to Taoism – both historically and in terms of its content. One of Zen's particular merits lies in its having absorbed Taoism on whose fertile soil it developed, bore, and is still bearing fruit, thereby keeping it alive as an active force. Alongside Zen Buddhism and Buddhism (inclusive of ancient Chinese and Taoist elements) Japan also adopted the basic principles of Confucian social theory and ethics. That is why Taoist influences are not always immediately recognisable – even for the Japanese themselves, who anyway tend to subsume under Zen anything that might derive from Taoist roots.

In true Kyūdō the meditative breathing practices aimed at mental and physical relaxation and concentration start long before the actual bow practice. Indeed, this basic meditative attitude is supposed to permeate every action or non-action, every thought, one's every manifestation at all hours of day and night, no matter what activity one may be engaged in at the time. If the discipline of Zen or Kyūdō remained restricted to the practice hall, the objective of training would not have been achieved.

The meditation is intended to help attainment of the stage of inner and outer stillness essential for the transformation process described above. As in all Budō sports and Zen arts, breathing is in principle abdominal; i.e. it relies on the action of the diaphragm. Shallow breathing, restricted to the thorax, is basically unnatural even though it has become 'second nature' for many people. Such shallow breathing quickly leads to fatigue and tension. It basically prevents any physical or mental relaxation, and obstructs the important consciously felt connection with the energies that surround us. Correct breathing aims solely at the conscious tapping, accumulation, and control of cosmic vital energies in the body.

The diaphragm occupies a central place in our body, and that is why it plays a key role in the respiratory process. This organ divides the body into two main sections, an upper one which essentially contains the heart and lungs, and a lower one with the intestines. The whole upper part of the body rests on the diaphragm, which consequently forms a link between the two sections. During inhalation it exerts a slight pressure downwards, causing the lower abdomen to arch outwards. The diaphragm drops while the whole abdomen expands, with the automatic result that the rib-cage also expands slightly so that air is drawn in and the circulation of the blood is kept going. The more air we take in, the more blood will be supplied to the lungs and the heart. During exhalation the diaphragm curves slightly upwards again and the lower abdomen is pulled in once more. The upward pressure of the diaphragm expels the stale air in the lungs after it has performed its function of cleansing the blood which has been drawn upwards for that purpose.

Another breathing practice which is often employed in Kyūdō and Za-zen begins with an exhalation whereby the diaphragm puts firm but not unnaturally strenuous pressure on the lower

31

abdomen, thus distributing the subtle vital energy throughout the body while the stale air is drawn off and released. The tension thus arising in the lower abdomen is maintained by refraining from breathing in for as long as there is no unnatural strain, and one can feel a beneficial effect on mind and body, calming, strengthening, and stabilizing them. Release of that tension coincides with inhalation because the diaphragm then automatically – without our volition being involved – exerts a slight upward pressure towards the navel, drawing in fresh air completely independently. When the abdomen and lungs are full, there is a brief pause before exhalation.

Experience has shown that after considerable practice more archers tend to adopt the second method in Kyūdō since the natural tension in the lower abdomen during exhalation is felt to lead to a more stabilising and strengthening build-up of energy, and the automatic inhalation due to the action of the diaphragm makes it easier to keep the upper and lower body in a firm but unforced balance. Because of its intermediate position in the body and its function in breathing and blood circulation, the diaphragm has often been called the 'second heart'. It is the organ that initiates our respiration, the exchange of oxygen, and circulation of the blood. It is continually in action and can only be slightly relaxed if the breath is held after each exhalation and inhalation. Hence the pleasant energy and calm during the retention of breath, which can be felt radiating from the lower abdomen, permeating the entire body and bringing peace to the mind.

This is where physical and mental concentration begin. The archer takes advantage of this so as to empty his mind of all disturbing influences whether they originate within himself or outside – and to align his body with the relaxed state of his mind. As far as the body itself is concerned, that primarily means that the muscles and bones are no longer felt as separate components but really as one tangible unity. In addition the breath has to find its own rhythm, and after just a few days that is no longer any problem. Once the archer has established this state of stillness within himself, he will – in the silence of his heart – be able to sense and hear the Tao within himself and without, above and below. When he picks up his bow, he must and will derive all his movements from this fundamental spiritual attitude – effortlessly and without excessive participation of the will, correctly but without calculation.

This state of calm and concentration persists without change.

The archer shoots without willing to shoot because that happens to be the activity he is engaged in. He could just as well be doing something else in the same spirit. And he hits the target – not because he wants to hit the target but because it is his task at that particular moment to bring the process of shooting an arrow to its natural conclusion. Strict discipline with years of bow practice and hard work on oneself is, however, indispensable for attainment of that high degree of unintentionality. The quality of breathing determines whether there is effortless rather than strained and willed self-control as well as a sure, apparently instinctive, mastery of the technique of archery.

Like Tantrism and Indian Yoga, Taoism distinguishes between different channels in which the breath circulates through the body, such as the automatic and the controlled, the ascending and the descending. Along the course of those pathways are to be found what are called psychic energy centres where cosmic energy is concentrated.[15] Meditative breathing helps one to become aware of the breath flowing through the body and to learn to control it. The subtle element of *ch'i* can be consciously directed as required to any of the psychic energy centres and to any part of the body. After several weeks of continuous practice, which must not, however, be restricted to training with the bow itself, that stage can be attained, making it possible to sense the circulation of the breath as a kind of current of heat. One will also be able to focus on any chosen psychic centre, directing the breath to it so as to accumulate psychic subtle energy there and channel it onwards.

The highest of these centres, called chakras in Yoga and Tantrism, lies behind the forehead exactly between the eyebrows. It is where Indian women place their caste mark. The lowest of these chakras is to be found at the bottom of the spine. The centre situated about 3 cm. below the navel is of prime importance in Japanese archery. Taoism calls this centre *ch'i-hai*, the ocean of breath. Japanese Zen has the same expression *(ki-kai)* but today it tends to use the more popular term *tanden*, a compound of the characters denoting 'red' and 'rice field'. The character for red is said to derive from alchemy's vermillion elixir of life in later Taoism, which – according to Taoist alchemists – can be distilled in the human body by way of different exercises, bestowing immortality. If one accepts that interpretation, the *tanden* would constitute the place in the human body where capacity for the attainment of immortality is situated. In that connection the sign for 'rice field' can easily be interpreted as 'life-giving field'. Even today, Japanese encyclopaedias maintain that health and courage result from directing one's energy into the *tanden*. The term *tanden* is at any rate indispensable in Kyūdō and the other martial arts.

The *tanden* is not only the centre where all the muscular impulses originate; as already mentioned, it is also very closely connected with the development of subtle energies of mind and body. When we direct attention to the *tanden*, we will immediately realise that even the slightest movement – say, of the legs, an arm, or the head – automatically arises there. That is not merely the lower abdomen muscles' reaction to movements by various parts of the body. Those movements originate there. We cannot cough, speak, or breathe without tensing the *tanden* muscles. If the *tanden* is strengthened by abdominal respiration – which although directed to begin with will later become completely automatic – the strength and precision of all other bodily movements will also improve. Whether directed or not, movements which are accompanied by abdominal breathing and firmly rooted in the *tanden* often exert great fascination on people who are not familiar with this breathing technique.

This centre is even more important with regard to the development of physical and spiritual (psychic) subtle energies, and to the control of one's own thought processes. That is due to the fact that this area in the lower abdomen constitutes a kind of resonant circuit with the brain forming the second important element. In this circuit subtle energies flow through our body and its nervous system. When we hold our breath after an exhalation or an inhalation, there will be instantaneous and inevitable tension in the *tanden*, immediately attracting our attention. We thus 'look' into the *tanden* with our inner eye, and our mind and thinking are thereby to a certain extent 'materialised' and made visible. Breath and thought merge into one. Anybody can employ that simple exercise in breath retention on any occasion and in any situation in order to gain fresh strength for coping with the demands of everyday life.

It is, of course, not to be disputed that the brain is the part of our body charged with the task of thinking and planning, occupying the position of a kind of 'control room'. The *tanden* muscle of the lower abdomen in conjunction with the diaphragm is, however, the first to implement impulses coming from the brain. If those two muscles were out of action, no plan conceived by the brain could be put into effect. When those muscles are working properly, subtle energies will be produced and set to work. The result of that activity is signalled to the brain, which then gives new orders. A cyclical process is thus set in motion. Mental activity takes place through the oscillation between the brain and the lower abdomen muscles participating in the respiratory process. Even emotions are expressed in that way. Laughter, fear, and worry can only manifest themselves if we activate the appropriate muscles in the abdomen. Each of those muscles plays a part in respiration. We will also only be able to control our thoughts and emotions if we bring about the appropriate state of tension in the lower abdomen's respiratory muscles by way of conscious abdominal breathing involving the diaphragm. Controlled breathing generates mental power; and attentiveness, which is nothing other than mental power, can never be achieved without tensing the lower abdominal muscles. The *tanden* itself does not serve any conscious function, but if we activate it as one of the two poles in the inner circuit of subtle energies, we endow it with some degree of spiritual power.[16]

The archer needs to concentrate primarily on this point. This is where every step, movement, and motion, as well as all awareness, have their origin and centre — right up to the moment when the arrow is released. In Kyūdō that also applies to every movement in the archer's everyday existence. All action and non-action originate in the *tanden*. That is why breathing must proceed from the *tanden*. Having made that physically perceptible and accessible for practical application in our everyday existence is just one of the achievements of Taoism, Zen, and Kyūdō. By seriously practising their techniques, we can increase well-being, enhance resilience, and sharpen mental powers. Taoism and Zen Buddhism speak of the *hara* (stomach) as the seat and centre of our thinking. The wise old men of ancient China called that 'thinking with the stomach'; Zen masters to this very day use that expression; and the Kyūdō teacher's recommendation to his pupil is 'to shoot with the stomach'. *Hara* is the seat and centre of all spiritual energies, which are concentrated in the *tanden. Tanden* breathing is therefore ultimately 'spiritual breathing'.

The first and most basic practice for anyone wanting to devote himself to Taoist meditation or to enter the Way of the Bow involves exact location of the *ch'i-hai* or *tanden* point in the *hara*. This point is situated about 3 cm. below the navel and can therefore be found without difficulty. What really matters, however, is to feel and *experience* it in a physically tangible way. Among the many techniques which are of use here, the following is considered to be one of the easiest. It is completely natural, and when practised properly it is infallible.

Keeping the body upright – the spine has to be absolutely vertical – one expels the air contained in the upper part of the lungs by slightly tensing the diaphragm so that it exerts some pressure upwards. Pausing briefly, one can immediately feel a pleasant emptiness in the chest. Ancient Kyūdō texts talk about a kind of 'void'. The chest takes on the character of an empty space. After this exhalation – which should be easy and without strain – some air will have remained in the lungs. One can now try to use up this residue by laughing rapidly and softly. That may sound strange, but if one tries this out for oneself, one will notice a slight tension in a particular part of the abdomen, giving rise to pleasant warmth or energy there. The ocean of breath, the *tanden*, has thus been located, and one can now focus attention on it when breathing.

Another equally simple method is as follows. One creates a pleasant stabilising tension in the abdomen by an even exhalation involving the diaphragm. About 20 per cent of the air should remain in the lungs. Next one attempts to swallow a little saliva. It will be noticed that the muscles of the lower abdomen tense in order to make the process of swallowing possible. The centre of this slight tension is once again the *tanden*. By employing the two methods in succession it will be possible to determine whether one really hit on the same spot both times.

Focusing on the centre of body and mind thus located, one now begins to take in an even but deep breath with assistance from the diaphragm. As soon as stomach and lungs are filled, one holds the breath without having to pay attention to the lungs. They will automatically have received enough air and oxygen once the stomach has been filled. The brief pause – during which concentration is not interrupted – increases the accumulation of cosmic subtle energy in the *tanden*. During the subsequent exhalation, the vital energy thus perceptibly gained can be directed to whatever part of the body may particularly need it in order to perform the specific step the archer is engaged in at the time – or to any other activity. That is done by directing the gaze of the inner eye onto that specific part. Exhalation should take about twice as long as inhalation, and also involve the action of the diaphragm. In this case the diaphragm will exert slight pressure either upwards or downwards, depending on which method has been chosen. When the air has been expelled, one pauses again and can now feel how a marvellously refreshing, agreeable calm spreads from the *tanden* to body and mind, bringing about a pleasant glow throughout. The whole respiratory process should amount to an absolutely even and natural flowing motion involving no exaggerated effort or outer direction. Its strength should primarily derive from a state of deep mental and physical collectedness. After some practice, this concentration will develop of its own accord and will no longer have to be consciously initiated. One should breathe softly like a child but without weakness – says Lao-tzu.

If the archer's breathing has been correct until the arrow leaves the bow, the sudden backward movement of the right hand, releasing the arrow and bowstring, will be checked by the vital energy concentrated in the *tanden*. The firmness and composure of the archer's posture will thus not be impaired by any sudden jolt. Concentration remains intact, the breath is discharged in a harmonious flow, and the essence of Kyūdō – the unity of body, mind, and bow – has been attained. It is self-evident that such a shot will hit its target, provided the archer's technique was without fault.

Slightly above the *tanden* is the navel. Following ancient tradition, my old Kyūdō teacher used to call it the 'Seat of God'. According to Taoism and Zen Buddhism, that of course stands for 'Nothingness', the Void (Jap. *ku*). Like the centre of a circle, the navel is the centre-point of the body. When concentration and meditation make that point really accessible to experience, it is transformed into a kind of centre of gravity. The tangible accumulation and materialisation of all spiritual and physical energies takes place, however, in the *tanden* just below the navel. It is there that the Void manifests itself as a highly active reality. The *tanden* is therefore the very core of the individual human being, the seat of true being in every single one of us. Abdominal breathing ensures that the psychic and cosmic vital energies do not just ascend through the navel into the upper part of the body during inhalation. That would result in a separation of upper and lower body, and any attempt at establishing a harmonious relationship between body and mind would be condemned to failure. With the *tanden* as the centre, those energies are evenly distributed upwards and downwards. In that way the upper and lower parts of the body maintain their natural unity.

The desperate and useless expenditure of energy which

beginners often display as they draw their bow – bringing to mind the pitiful spectacle of a fish struggling helplessly when out of its element – is in most cases caused by loss of contact with the central point of the *tanden*. Upper and lower body have been separated by inadequate breathing. Beginners often try to draw their bow during a forceful inhalation, but they cannot succeed because the psychic vital energy mainly develops during exhalation and breath retention. Since the Kyūdō bow – unlike the Western archery bow – does not possess any mechanical aids, it is not possible to compensate for any such inadequacy by means of purely external technical adjustments. All really strenuous movements in Kyūdō are accompanied not by an in-breath but by either an even exhalation or by retention of one's breath in the ocean of breath. That is done in order to allow increased development and accumulation of natural tension and energies to take place there. Those energies can then be directed along the appropriate channels towards those parts of the body especially in need of them at that moment. Since the *tanden* always remains the centre of gravity for body and mind, the central focus in the respiratory process, the arrow is only outwardly released by the right hand which had been holding the drawn bowstring. The real discharge comes from the *tanden*. The instinctive impulse that brings about the shot has its origin there and not in the brain, let alone the arm or hand, which only serve an executive function.

During all the movements involved, the breathing continues to be calm, deep, and even, at one with the rhythm pulsating through the universe. It could be compared to a gentle but steady breeze blowing across a patch of sand without disturbing the tiniest grain. Such breathing resembles that of a new born child. It is deep and unconscious, never feeble and hesitant, full of a will to live. It rises and falls evenly like an unbroken column of mercury, ascending whilst continuing to rest firmly on its core. An arrow discharged in that spirit and in conjunction with this breath is an impressive illustration of the ancient principle of Kyūdō, captured in the words 'Motion in stillness'. The mental attitude rests on union of mind and body, and on their active integration in the energies of the cosmos. It is achieved through the spiritualisation of breathing, which in the Way of the Bow is employed as a form of meditation. Consciousness has to focus on the respiratory process and become quietly absorbed in it. After some practice, all directed seeking for the correct breathing technique becomes superfluous. Focused and spiritualised energy acting in conjunction with complete mindfulness and uttermost natural concentration result in the archer's actions automatically initiating the appropriate breathing.

Taoism and Zen start out from the premiss that the living rhythms of the universe also permeate the rhythms of our bodies and minds. The rhythm of our respiration can bring us into harmony with cosmic rhythms. The fact that we can regulate and direct our breathing rhythm is a gift from heaven. We are ourselves masters of the process of integration and self-realisation, irrespective of the favour or disfavour of any God or gods. The only preconditions are persistence, strict self-discipline, and unerring self-control.

What really matters during inhalation, breath retention, exhalation, and renewed retention is to become aware of our individual rhythm, understanding and concretely experiencing its interaction with the cosmic rhythm so that they will ultimately achieve alignment and become one. Kyūdō also demands of the archer that all his movements – up to release of the arrow and the moment when he steps back from the shooting line – be harmonised with the unified individual and cosmic rhythm. That may appear to be difficult, but after sufficient practice it really takes care of itself in the most natural way. Anyone who breathes correctly and has achieved the decisive re-fusion of those two poles, which originally constituted a unity and were only rent asunder by our self-centredness and the illusion of possession of a separate I, cannot help but attain perfection in execution of all the movements required by the technique of archery. He will integrate these movements into the 'Great Harmony', the 'Great Breath'. Once the archer has acquired the correct technique through persistent practice and learnt to breathe in the right way so that he can let technique and breath look after themselves – allowing them to arise out of his innermost being and to manifest as they wish, all his actions will start in the 'Great Harmony', the Tao, and the archer has attained his goal.

Kyūdō is of use and value in a further respect. The level of development achieved by an archer will be made immediately apparent both to himself and an observer by the way in which he handles bow and arrow. As a form of meditation, Kyūdō is at the same time something very practical, being both active and creative. Since both aspects, the contemplative and the active, have to stand the test of the immediate moment in concrete reality, every shot is an immense test for the archer. Although he is taking action, he has to stand unmoved in the *wu-wei*, in Non-Doing. Out of that Non-Doing he has to actively discharge his arrow. Such a shot often arouses an almost magical fascination in the observer. This is due to the archer's masterly technique, his correct abdominal breathing, and especially the wide-awake abandonment to his inner space from where the arrow is released almost automatically as that centre opens itself to the all-pervading powers of the universe.

The Way and the Ways

The term Kyūdō is made up of the Sino-Japanese expression for bow *(kyū)* – in modern Japanese *yumi* and in ancient times *tarashi* (from *toru*, taking in one's hand) – and the Sino-Japanese character for *dō*, which is read as Tao in Chinese, as *michi* in Japanese, and roughly means way or path.

Compounds with dō (also pronounced tō) are relatively frequent in Japanese, including Kendō (Way of the Sword), Jūdō (the Yielding Way), Kadō (Way of the Flower), Chadō or Sadō (Way of Tea), Shōdō (Way of Writing), Karate-dō (Way of the Empty Hand), Shintō (Way of the Gods, i.e. Shintoism, the original religion in ancient Japan), Bushidō (Way of the Warrior), Dōkyō (Religion of the Way, i.e. Taoism), Zendō (Zen Way, i.e. Zen Buddhism), and last but not least Kyūdō (Way of the Bow).

The literal meaning of Tao, dō (tō), and *michi* is way or path, but alternative translations such as the Absolute, the Principle, the Law, and Nature can also be justified. The derivation of the word *dō* from Tao points to China, and the classic definition is to be found in Lao-tzu's *Tao-te-ching (Tao-te-king)*. The founder of Taoism says there:

> The Tao that can be told is not the eternal Tao.
> The name that can be named is not the eternal name.
> The nameless is the beginning of heaven and earth.
> The named is the mother of ten thousand things.[1]

Tao there signifies the source of all being and the way of the universe. In that sense Tao also means:

> . . . The Road or Way in which the Universe moves, its methods

and processes, its conduct and operation, the complex of phenomena regularly recurring in it, in short, the Order of the World, Nature, or Natural Order. It actually is in the main the annual rotation of the seasons producing the process of growth, or renovation and decay; it may accordingly be called Time, the creator and destroyer.[2]

The Tao or way of the universe has its correspondence in the Tao as the way of man. The way of man must harmonise as completely as possible with the way of the cosmos. If man therefore deviates in his thoughts and actions from the way of the universe to which he is subordinate, he will inevitably come into conflict with himself and the surrounding world. Later we shall explore in more detail how man can fulfil his personal Tao and thereby the Tao of the cosmos.

At any rate, from that viewpoint it becomes understandable that the term 'Way' was specifically adopted by a variety of arts and sciences since the arts include everything that contributes to the perfection of human nature and furthers man's aspiration to complete self-realisation.

Although the concept of dō has been known in Japan at least since the *Kojiki*, the first surviving work of history (completed in AD 712), and the *Nihonshoki (Nihongi,* AD 720), a considerable time passed before its original meaning was more or less understood there and began to be used accordingly. Before the Nara Period (AD 710 – 784) the word only referred to the pursuit of crafts and intellectual skills. Japanese understanding of the 'Way' gradually began to change though. That process got under way in the sixth century when relations and exchanges with the Chinese mainland were intensified, and China's various philosophical systems, some dating back for thousands of years, were studied in more detail. Taoism, Buddhism, Confucianism, and the age-old Yin–Yang teaching made a particular contribution to the development of a new understanding of the Way towards the end of the Nara era. That understanding increasingly involved moral and ethical considerations, relating man and all of his action and inaction to the universe and its powers of Yin-Yang and *ch'i*. Man was from then on viewed as deriving from the universe and its all-pervading powers. The *Nihongi* in particular contains numerous examples of that attitude.

Aiming at the harmonisation of man's actions with the laws of the universe, the Way thus provides man with principles

41

regulating his entire life. During the Heian Period (794–1185) that interpretation and application of the term 'Way' was given a kind of official underpinning when the more powerful aristocratic clans increasingly developed a stronger sense of tradition. Ever since that time, it has become an established aspect of practical and intellectual life in Japan. During the Heian Period all kinds of Ways began to proliferate since all scholarly activities and arts acquired that status. The decisive consolidation and perfection of those Ways only took place during the Kamakura Period (1192–1333). At that time the spiritual aspect of the Way came to the fore. As a result the Way was no longer only of significance for specialists in a particular art or science but could also offer the layman a sense of direction and a model for his everyday existence.

The exclusivity of the Way was thus ended. The Way became accessible to broader sections of the population, thereby developing into a kind of educational tool capable of furthering man's self-perfecting in the entirety of his thought, action, and feeling. The guidelines were provided by the principles and creative energies of the cosmos.

That is how the concept of the 'Way' became one of the fundamental ideas within practical and intellectual life in Japan, thereby exerting a profoundly formative and pervasive impact on the establishment of individual disciplines in the arts, philosophy, and religion as well as on many areas of everyday existence.[3] That impact is largely explained by the influence of Zen Buddhism, which succeeded in establishing itself extensively during the Kamakura Period. During the Sung era (960–1279) Japan had reactivated trade relations with China which had come to a virtual standstill at the end of the T'ang Period. The Japanese initiative mainly came from feudal lords and the powerful monasteries since state power was largely decentralised at that time. The monasteries were of course interested in cultural as well as commercial opportunities, extending to Chinese literature, art, philosophy, and religion. Japan thus became familiar with Chinese ideas to an extent hitherto unknown. Zen, which was already in decline in China, held a particular attraction. The adoption of Chinese ideas was primarily promoted by what were known as the Gozan monasteries (Jap. *gozan*, 'five mountains', in this context the most important Zen monasteries), which included the Teryūji, Shōkokuji, Kenninji, Tōfukuji, and Manjūji monasteries in Kyōto, and the Kenchōji, Engakuji, Jufukuji,

Jōchiji, and Jōmyōji monasteries in Kamakura. In 1386 the great Nanzenji monastery at Kyōto was endowed with authority over them.

The first Japanese Zen masters, such as Eisai Zenji (1141-1215) and his disciple Dogen Zenji (1200-1253), had received their crucial training in China during the Sung Dynasty. Japan's first contact with Zen (Chin. *Ch'an*) nevertheless dates back to the Nara Period (eighth century), when Japanese monks travelled to China, and to the beginning of the ninth century, when a Chinese Zen Buddhist monk, known in Japan as Gikū, tried to spread Zen teachings at Heian-kyō (today's Kyōto), the Japanese capital at that time. Gikū's efforts were not completely in vain. Egaku, a Japanese monk, became his follower and visited the Chinese Empire in 858 in order to learn more about this school of Buddhism. After his return, he too tried to establish Zen in Japan but without appreciable success.

It must be remembered that when China adopted Zen Buddhism, it could already look back on a highly developed civilisation extending over thousands of years. When Japan first came into contact with Zen ideas, its culture was still relatively rudimentary. Until well into the eighth century, Japan was simply not sufficiently receptive for such radically new ideas. Too much else had to be assimilated first. The fourth century had seen the introduction of Confucian thought, and orthodox Buddhism had been brought in during the sixth century.[4]

Today Eisai Zenji is regarded as the man who really established Zen in Japan. In 1202 he founded one of the later Gozan monasteries at Kyōto, the Kenninji monastery which belonged to the Rinzai (Chin. Lin-chi) school. His disciple Dogen Zenji later set up the Eiheiji monastery, which has remained the centre of the Sōtō (Chin. *Ts'ao-tung*) school to this day. In China Zen merged over the course of time with its most important precursor, Taoism, and also with the Pure Land school of Buddhism, gradually losing its importance as a cultural force, particularly because of its contact with the latter. In Japan, however, Zen permeated the whole of cultural life and gained access to many areas of everyday existence from the Kamakura Period onwards.

Zen established itself as the most important school of Japanese Buddhism as early as the Ashikaga epoch (1333-1573). That was mainly the outcome of Zen's teachings, but other more peripheral historical factors and specific aspects of the Japanese character also favoured that development. In 1325 the Japanese

Government sent an official delegation to China for the first time in 500 years. In 1279 the Mongols had conquered the southern Sung Dynasty, leading many Chinese Zen monks to flee to Japan where they sought refuge for themselves and their teachings. That fact played a decisive part in the flowering of Zen in Japan. As already mentioned, the most famous Japanese Zen masters of that time had been significantly influenced by what they had learnt in China, and had helped to intensify cultural links between the two countries. Many Japanese Zen masters were also successful in gaining influence among Japanese government circles — with Musō Soseki (or Musō Kokushi, 1275–1351) being the outstanding example.

During the reign of the Ashikaga Shōguns, who had close links with Zen Buddhism or the associated arts, Zen monks gained influence over the Japanese educational system since administration of the temple schools (Terakoya) was in their hands. The head of the Ashikaga Academy was also a Zen priest. In addition, Zen priests acted as advisors to the Ashikaga with regard to foreign trade, which mainly involved business with the Chinese mainland. After the Ming Dynasty (1368–1644) had gained power there, Japanese monks made special efforts to promote Chinese culture in Japan and headed the trade missions sent to China. Finally, Zen priests provided the Shōguns with advice on artistic matters. Japan experienced a period of unprecedented cultural development, especially under the Ashikaga rulers – simultaneously accompanied by political conflicts and military struggle.

Unsuccessful Mongol attempts at invasion of Japan in 1274 and 1281 led, among other things, to the adoption of Zen throughout the warrior class. The emphasis on practicalities and the *Mushin* technique (Jap. *mushin*, mental detachment) particularly appealed to the Samurai since that contributed towards perfection of their military prowess and helped them tolerate a harsh warrior existence. The down-to-earth Samurai also appreciated Zen's rejection of all accentuation of theory and its emphasis on immediate experience. The warriors' tactics had proved relatively unsuccessful during the Mongols' first assault in 1274, before Zen had become properly established in their ranks. Highly formal notions about honourable man-to-man combat were useless in a confrontation with the disciplined formations of Mongol soldiers, contributing precious little to the enemy's final withdrawal.

From that time on, the Samurai life-style and their military tactics were crucially dominated by the Zen notion that all action has to be spontaneous and unpremeditated, like a reflex, leaving no room for thought. Not even the slightest thought of victory or defeat, life or death, was allowed to establish itself in the warrior's mind since that would have affected the immediacy of his intuitive mindfulness. As a result, the Samurai achieved some considerable successes during the second Mongol invasion, although once again the Kamikaze, the heavenly winds, ultimately tipped the scales in their favour.

The flourishing of culture during the politically unstable Ashikaga Period also led many writers, artists, and scholars to flee to monasteries, especially Zen foundations. They hoped to be able to pursue their work in peace there. Contacts with China were undoubtedly the decisive factor in the amazing rise of Zen in Japan. Such contacts would not, however, have born such fruit without that attitude of openness and curiosity about everything new and unknown which is a basic characteristic of the Japanese character. Only that can completely explain the enthusiasm for everything foreign and the prestige it enjoys in Japanese society. In the Japan of that time 'foreign countries' meant first and foremost China. Compared with China, Japan still had very far to go. The cultural impulses that came from China thus had sufficient scope for development in Japan except at times of utter satiation. The naive simplicity of Shintō, Japan's nature religion whose roots reach back to prehistoric times, may have contributed to the adoption of Chinese Zen. Alongside Buddhism, Shintō with its closeness to nature and the powers at work there, has remained, to this day, the most important religion in Japan. It is not therefore surprising that many Japanese were particularly disposed towards assimilating a religion like Chinese Zen whose main features — simplicity, rejection of everything superfluous and bombastic, and emphasis on what is natural, small, and inconspicuous – were very similar to Shintō.

But to return to the concept of the Way. This concept, which derived from Yin–Yang teachings, Taoism, Confucianism, and later adoption by Chinese Ch'an (Zen), has not been philosophically further elaborated since being brought to Japan by Japanese monks. It was, however, resolutely implemented there. Hence it is in Japan today – more accurately *only* in Japan – that we can still study its practical application in the most diverse spheres of the arts, sciences, and everyday life. What is even more important, we can ourselves gain practical experience by personal study of one of the relevant disciplines such as Kyūdō. Obviously, it can hardly be maintained that the Taoist or Zen Buddhist notion of the Way is still actively alive in modern China, even though more recent reports suggest that certain Taoist ideas continue to lead a hidden existence there. To have kept this concept alive so that anybody can experience its true meaning in a tangible way even today is an inestimable gift and achievement of Japanese culture. Thus the 'Ways' continue to exist amidst the depressing industrial devastation, the unimaginable noise, and nearly total mechanisation of the big cities, accompanied by an increasingly dangerous loss of direction among much of today's youth. The 'Ways' can still be pursued and practised in little old temples or private buildings often squeezed between high-rise blocks belonging to some mammoth enterprise or other. What has come down through the ages thus unerringly continues in existence. It may be under pressure but it has at any rate not yet been eliminated.

Even though all the previously mentioned 'Ways' originated in ancient China, they were not directly pursued there as practical paths towards self-knowledge. They primarily served as complementary, supportive measures in conjunction with meditation and other practices designed to lead to the Self. John Blofeld, for example, tells us about Taoist monks and hermits who resorted to the practice of archery, swordsmanship, or flower arranging whenever they felt that might profit their studies or meditation.[5] It was left to the Japanese to cultivate those practices as independent Ways and as traditions which were passed on from generation to generation, from master to disciple, and further developed over the course of time. All the essential ideas were, however, already present in the Chinese understanding of the Way, especially the notion that the Way ultimately entails discovering and becoming one with the Great Truth, the principle of the universe, which is active within every single one of us. That applies to all individual disciplines of the Way from the Art of Tea to the Way of the Bow.

Tao, Zen, and Archery

At the very heart of Taoist teaching is the concept of the Void.

46

That applies to both the genesis of the world and cosmos, and to man's transformation within the world and cosmos. Chuang-tzu says in his 12th chapter:

> In the great beginning, there was non-being. It had neither being nor name. The One originates from it: it has oneness but not yet physical form. When things obtain it and come into existence, that is called virtue [which gives them their individual character]. That which is formless is divided [into Yin and Yang], and from the very beginning going on without interruption is called destiny [ming, fate]. Through movement and rest it produces all things. When things are produced in accordance with the principle [Li] of life, there is physical form. When the physical form embodies and preserves the spirit so that all activities follow their own specific principles, that is nature. By cultivating one's nature one will return to virtue. When virtue is perfect, one will be one with the beginning. Being one with the beginning, one becomes vacuous [hsu, receptive to all], and being vacuous one becomes great. One will then be united with the sound and breath of things. When one is united with the sound and breath of things, one is then united with the universe. The unity is intimate and seems to be stupid and foolish. This is called profound and secret virtue, this is complete harmony.[1]

Non-being, the great all-embracing void, the Tao, already contains all potential creation. From it springs the One, which is not yet visible. The One divides itself into Yin and Yang, the female and the male creative principles whose interaction in repose (Yin) and movement (Yang) brings forth all beings and things. Man's Way should be directed towards regaining his original state, the state of unity, of the great void and the primeval Tao. He has to become completely empty.

This process of inner evolution is of fundamental significance. It determines the adequacy of our actions in the real world, and is crucial for our everyday existence whose aim is to find happiness, contentment, freedom, and inner peace. The inestimable value of Taoist and Zen ideas lies in their relatedness to tangible reality. But why is this process of inner evolution of such importance to man? After all, one might object, such evolution is seen here in relation to the universe, even before the world came into being – and can therefore hardly be of relevance for the everyday reality of human existence.

In the chapter on breath and breathing, mention was made of

the Chinese view that man is an organic, integral part of the cosmos with every single one of his manifestations directly interacting with cosmic powers. Man also constitutes the cosmos. We and all things carry the cosmos within ourselves and the cosmos bears us within itself. To return to the state of primeval unity, the Void, essentially means no more nor less than to take part in creation itself. From the beginning every being carries that possibility within itself, but we humans have filled our minds and being to the brim with thousands of meaningless superficialities, with irrelevant views, desires, and ideas, so that there is no room left. That potential, although still present, is thus hopelessly buried and repressed in most people.

For Chuang-tzu becoming 'empty' does not mean anything at all negative but rather something extremely positive, namely to become receptive and open to everything that is of real importance. In the 11th chapter of his Tao-te-ching, Lao-tzu illustrates this positive significance of the Void in a very striking way:

> Thirty spokes share the wheel's hub;
> It is the centre hole that makes it useful.
> Shape clay into a vessel;
> It is the space within that makes it useful.
> Cut doors and windows for a room;
> It is the hole which makes it useful.
> Therefore profit comes from what is there;
> Usefulness from what is not there.[2]

The wheel derives its usefulness from the fact that there are no spokes in the hub, which is hollow. Although the spokes do not extend into the central empty space of the hub, their essence does. In the same way, a container is useful only inasmuch as the material from which it is made encloses an empty space. It is precisely the emptiness created by the form which constitutes the vessel's essence. Only thanks to that emptiness can we use it. The same applies to the windows and doors of a house. All being is simultaneously non-being. Man is no exception. Only by becoming 'empty', empty and free from all irrelevant influences, desires, and ideas, will we be able to know ourselves, and, reconciled with the powers of the cosmos, shape our lives in harmony and peace with ourselves and the surrounding world.

Helplessness, emotional instability, and inner restlessness are principally caused by our ridiculous attempts to suppress dissatisfaction by time and again trying to bury it beneath superficialities. As a result, we are often tormented by frenzied consumerism, alcoholism, and drug addiction alongside egoism, self-seeking, and intolerance. Most people are simply incapable of admitting to themselves, or of acting in accordance with, what they have actually known for a long time: that all such superficial distractions lead nowhere in the end, and that the fulfilment of one desire inevitably awakens another, thus creating a fatally never-ending chain. In the course of this self-destructive process, man's ability to listen to the voice of his true Self will be weakened to such an extent that he will ultimately succumb to self-deception, taking all his superficial cravings and desires as expressions of that real Self. Lao-tzu comments in that connection:

> The five colours blind the eye.
> The five tones deafen the ear.
> The five flavours dull the taste.
> Racing and hunting madden the mind.
> Precious things lead one astray.
>
> Therefore the sage is guided by what he feels
>   and not by what he sees.
> He lets go of that and chooses this.[3]

Anyone who gorges himself on all such distractions and sensuous pleasures remains chained to his outer little I and cannot penetrate his inner space so as to fulfil his true destiny – because that demands becoming empty and free of all superficialities and all cravings. We should not let ourselves be guided by what we see – and that refers to the cravings of all the senses. What really matters, if heart and mind are to attain and preserve inner peace and clarity, is to empty oneself of everything that others might covet, possess, or shine with in the world. That is why the seeker focuses his attention inwards onto the stomach, which in Chinese and Japanese thought denotes the seat of the soul, the centre of the whole body.

The true seeker has to choose 'this', meaning whatever serves him well on his Way, and let go of 'that', meaning everything else. That is also what is signified when Zen master Sekiso says:

> Stop all your hankerings; let the mildew grow on your lips; make yourself like unto a perfect piece of immaculate silk; let your one

thought be eternity; let yourself be like dead ashes, cold and lifeless; again let yourself be like an old censer in a deserted village shrine.[4]

In a similar context Suzuki quotes another Zen sage:

Have no stirrings in your mind; be perfectly serene toward the objective world. To remain thus all the time in absolute emptiness and calmness is the way to be with the Buddha.[5]

Our entire inner being, our thinking and bodily sensations, have to be as clear and untarnished as a mirror without the least speck of dust on it. It must not be moved by anything – being like dead ashes, apparently cold and lifeless, apparently without particular function, useless like an old incense vessel in a deserted village temple.

Through this emptiness and freedom from all superficialities, the seeker ultimately attains union with the Buddha whom every human being carries within. Buddhism starts from the premiss that there is no God outside human reality, and the Buddha nature, which is ultimately nothing but the final reality of our own being, can be uncovered and activated within ourselves by means of certain disciplines. By contemplating nothingness – 'let eternity be your only thought' – our cosmic consciousness is uncovered. All our outer passions, all deadening ballast, fall away from us. We come to terms with ourselves; our reserves of inner strength are liberated; and we are no longer in conflict with ourselves. Our buried spiritual and cosmic consciousness, which is part of the power pervading the entire universe, is set free. Concentration and meditation develop our mind and substance, allowing our self to dissolve into the cosmic power. We return to the source and become part of cosmic energy since we humans are microcosmic beings reflecting the macrocosmos.

When Bodhidarma, who had come to India from China, met Emperor Wu of the Liang Dynasty (502–549) and was asked about the ultimate and holiest principle of his teaching, the man who was later to be viewed as the first patriarch of Zen is said to have answered: 'The vastness of the Void and nothing holy in it.' That may sound negative and possibly even nihilistic, but it is not in the very least so. Taoism, and even more clearly and concretely Zen, always strive to grasp the essence of all living things, the world in its totality, and life from within, thereby comprehending the cosmic unity of all being. Nothingness, Bodhidarma's 'vastness of the Void', does not mean renunciation of the world, and in no way involves protest and despair. Nor does it signify the transcending of an abyss, a notion that runs through much of Christian metaphysics. In Taoism and Zen, nothingness is the innermost essential condition of all things. It is Void and Abundance at the same time, and intimately linked with practical action.[6] That is why it is not only Zen monks who practice the Way, but also poets, artists, all kinds of sportsmen, growers of flowers, scholars, and soldiers (as the chapter on Bushidō will demonstrate).

The communal recitation of sūtras in Zen monasteries is to be understood as a form of meditation. It is intended to serve as mental preparation or support for the periods of actual silent meditation. The following lines from the *Prajñāpāramitā-Hridaya-Sūtra* are daily recited in most Zen monasteries even today:

> Thus, Sāriputra, all things have the character of emptiness, they have no beginning, no end, they are faultless and not faultless, they are not perfect and not imperfect. Therefore, o Sāriputra, here in this emptiness there is no form, no perception, no name, no concepts, no knowledge. No eye, no ear, no nose, no tongue, no body, no mind. No form, no sound, no smell, no taste, no touch, no objects. . . There is no knowledge, no ignorance, no destruction of ignorance . . . There is no decay nor death; there are no four truths, viz. there is no pain, no origin of pain, and no path to the stoppage of pain. There is no knowledge of Nirvāna, no obtaining of it, no not-obtaining of it. Therefore, o Sāriputra, as there is no obtaining of Nirvāna, a man who has approached the Prajñāparamitā of the Bodhisattvas dwells unimpeded in consciousness. When the impediments of consciousness are annihilated, then he becomes free of all fear, is beyond the reach of change, enjoying final Nirvāna.[7]

That quotation may serve as a concentrated summary of all that has been said so far. Attention should be focused on the human being who has become one with the Tao, with emptiness. Unimpeded by any manifestation of the outer consciousness he dwells in 'total awareness'. That state of perfect mindfulness allows him to grasp the essence of all things directly without the mediation of discursive thought. On that basis, his action will be spontaneous and in perfect accordance with the demands of whatever the situation may be. His mental state of emptiness and purity is in harmony with all the conditions of daily existence, which keeps him from losing touch with reality and treating life as a kind of exercise in metaphysics. His body has become an instrument to be used by the cosmic energies at work in him, just as he himself can make instrumental use of those cosmic energies.

With regard to Kyūdō, that state of perfect mindfulness is of the uttermost importance – both for the technical aspects of the process of discharging an arrow, and for the mental-spiritual attitude of the archer himself. As will be seen in the chapter on 'Spirit and Technique', those aspects constitute an inseparable unity. The state of unimpeded total awareness gives the archer the ability to discharge the arrow correctly by concentrating exclusively on the various motions and manipulations involved – without the conscious volition of his lower self, imprisoned in the illusion of I-ness, being necessary. That in turn demands of the archer that there should not be the least pause between the initiating impulse and his action. The impulse and its realisation coincide; the individual movements are to be seen as a harmonious whole, as a mighty river flowing tranquilly and majestically towards its destination, overcoming all obstacles in its path.

Such an archer is free of all premeditation, deliberate correction of his actions, or any other intentional effort. His shooting flows freely from his deepest inner centre, his own Void. It flows from that point in his being where he is connected with the macrocosmic energies, so that everything he does is permeated by the deepest genuine awareness. He is holding the bow, yet he does not hold it; he has become free of that piece of bamboo with its string. Even though he is making use of it, his action is not guided by his will and discursive thought but by the great principle which encompasses all being and non-being. That is the meaning of the following poem by a master of the Kamakura period:

> The bow is broken
> Arrows are all gone –
> This critical moment:
> No fainting heart cherish,
> Shoot with no delay.[8]

An archer at the stage of total awareness or 'motionless realisation' as Suzuki calls it elsewhere (it could also be termed 'holistic perception'[9]) has undoubtedly reached the point where the mastery obtained through the Way of the Bow will manifest itself and prove its worth in any situation. He remains a master even outside the archery hall (Jap. *dōjō*). Both the release of the arrow and all his other actions will be performed in harmony with the powers arising out of the concretely experienced Void. Whatever he does, it will be performed out of a state of total awareness, which he will try to maintain at all times. Archery in the Kyūdō hall is nothing less than a way of achieving that through practice. It is not just in the Kyūdō hall either that this attitude is put to the test. It has to manifest itself much more intensely and decisively in the reality of everyday existence. Practice with the bow must never become an end in itself, but has to remain what it is: a means and method for cleansing ourselves of everything superfluous and superficial by allowing it to fall away through the practice of archery, so that we become empty for the great Plenitude of our true inner space, the deeper layers of our Self.

An archer who has attained that level will have done years of untiring training. He will have directed his attention equally much towards techniques and physical skill, and towards the disciplining of his mind. Viewed outwardly, he will have grappled all those years with his bow, the rules governing archery technique, and their implications for bodily movements and posture. At the same time he will have endeavoured from the very beginning to raise his skill in the handling of bow and arrow above the purely technical level because he will have discovered after only a few training sessions that mastery of technique and hitting the target are not the sole purpose involved. He will have learned that he above all needs to shed his ambition and will-force in order to experience any progress in even the least detail of his technical handling of the bow and to approach the stage of total awareness and holistic perception.

In Kyūdō one form of ambition entails consciously hitting the target in order to demonstrate to others or to oneself what has already been achieved. Hitting the target *is* of crucial importance, and missing it amounts to a definite failure at that moment. What is unacceptable, however, is desire expressing the impulses of our superficial I. Such intentional willing prevents purposelessness and the integration of our Self within the Tao. It blocks holistic perception and leads to poor and chance hits. Unintentionality and sureness are intimately linked in Kyūdō. Realisation and experience of that purposelessness involve experiencing the great emptiness in ourselves, involve deep self-knowledge and self-identity.

When practised correctly, Kyūdō gives the archer an opportunity of attaining that realisation by way of tangible action in using bow and arrow – as a living, real experience surpassing all idle talk which will only intensify illusion – whilst he remains positively and actively at rest within himself.

In the literature about Taoism and Buddhism a variety of expressions are used to designate the I which prevents all self-knowledge, and the true I into whose depths we penetrate after successfully shattering the armour with which the negative I discourages and prevents us from getting that far. Most of the those expressions are quite apposite, and differences between them only reflect the cultural, intellectual, religious, or scholarly background of the different authors. The I which constitutes the obstacle is designated by such terms as ego-I, little I, delusory I, relative I, empirical I, and many others. The positive I is called the deeper I, deeper Self, true I, true Self, great I, absolute I, transcendent I, Buddha-nature, or Buddha-being. The term 'Self' does not usually designate our little, outer I, at least not without a corresponding attribute. 'Self' and 'I' are mostly used for our deeper Self in conjunction with an appropriate characterisation. A distinction is always made between I and Self. Deeper insight into our I can lead to realisation of the Self. Hence the Self is the more comprehensive.

At the stage of total awareness of which the *Prajñāpāramitā-Hridaya-Sūtra* (Jap. *Hannya-haramita-shingyō*) speaks, man has overcome one of humanity's greatest delusions. That delusion makes us mistake the little, empirical I, the delusory I, for the Transcendental Self. That is at the root of our ambition and egoism; leads to conflict, contempt, and oppression of other people; and to disharmony and discontent within ourselves. The little I is limited, relative, lacks freedom, and is conditioned by innumerable factors. It is continually at war with its environment, categorically feeling that justice is on its side. The little I is under the misapprehension that it is basically free but restricted in its 'free' development by what is not itself, by its environment and the many other relative 'I's in it. The outer life of the little I is thus determined by fluctuations in the preconditions for its existence, and its context is the world of 'multiplicity'. Inwardly, however, the empirical I experiences constant, direct, and total exchange with the Self, the transcendental I – as D. T. Suzuki explains in what is considered one of the clearest accounts of this matter.[10]

The transcendental I or Self manifests itself through the empirical I and dwells in it. Or even more clearly: the transcendental I needs the empirical I in order to embody itself in form. It is only through this form that it can become active. Even though the empirical self exists in total dependence on the Transcendental Self, that does not mean that we can simply get rid of our little, empirical I in order to penetrate to the true Self – as some Zen and Yoga texts seem to suggest. We cannot simply disconnect the transcendental from the empirical I so that the latter can contemplate the former since both are so intimately linked that one *is* the other. They are one and yet they are not one. All we can do is to try and understand their relationship. The delusion of which we spoke previously has its origin in a mistaken understanding of this very relationship.

Our true I is to be found where there is as yet no distinction between heaven and earth, where Yin and Yang have not yet emerged from the Tao, where the Tao is still undivided and resting in itself. Our little I is nevertheless a reality like any other reality, and no meditation, no archery aiming at 'conquering' this I, will ever lead to success. The good thing about meditation is just meditation. The bird in the sky does not think about having to flap its wings either. It simply flies. In meditation as in archery there should never be an intended aim. You meditate in order to meditate, and you use your bow simply in order to use it. The point is to immerse ourselves unconditionally in the relationship between our little I and our real I, to enter into the relationship between ourselves and the universe, the great oneness which connects us with the cosmos and the cosmos with us. They are one and the same, and yet different. By meditating in this way, by using our bow in this fashion, we will find after years of hard training that the tyranny of the little I and its drives will fall away of its own accord. Whatever the discipline we are practising it will be hard and relentless, but it has to be pursued without the compulsion of wanting to achieve something. In that way we will deprive our little I of its last refuge. As Alan Watts rightly points out, the last place of refuge of this little I is the intention to 'get rid of it'.

The person who practises with calm purposelessness and undivided attention, acting out of that abundant emptiness, recognises himself or herself in all things and in all other human beings. The wall between himself and his environment disappears, and the little ego loses its dominance, remaining limited to its natural functions. When the archer has released the arrow and watches it fly towards the target, the stage he has attained on this Way is revealed to him in a very direct and tangible manner. The trajectory of his arrow is a tangible demonstration to both himself and others of his own inner state. Some archers and authors maintain that our little I flies off with the arrow in the direction of the target. If that is meant or understood in the sense that a successful shot would rid us of our relative I, that we could force it to disappear for ever together with the arrow, we succumb to a fatal error. That I does not fly off with the arrow, but we will have experienced and tangibly demonstrated by such a shot that the little I no longer obstructs us, is no longer in charge of us, since we have understood its real function, and allow it to perform that function but no more than that.

Practitioners of Kyūdō are particularly prone to succumbing to the danger of self-delusion since outer combat and actual opponents seem to be completely lacking, unlike in Kendō, Jūdō, and most other martial arts. That leads many bowmen to make a mystique of the so-called 'inner fight', the combat against oneself – usually because the archer is incapable of conducting such an inner combat adequately, i.e. without intentionality and compulsion. Perfect technical skill in the handling of bow and arrow in a state of unintentionality demands incredible energy, effort, and endurance, both mentally and physically, because the Way is attained through the body. According to Taoism and Buddhism, mind and body are one. Essence and form are basically inseparable. Romantically illusory contentment with the level of one's inner combat and mere theorising are not infrequently found among Kyūdō archers. One of the causes is over-emphasis on the spiritual aspect, just because there is no outer adversary. On the other hand, the archer whose motives are purely external, striving to hit the target as substitute for an opponent, will at most achieve a high degree of outer skill.

The aim of any human Way as conceived by Taoism and Zen Buddhism is to act without thought or intentional doing – as a bud blossoms forth or a ripe fruit bursts open. 'Non-Thinking' and 'Non-Doing' are the means and method serving that purpose. 'Non-Thinking' does not, however, entail a state of absent-minded torpor. It is instead a kind of thinking which requires a maximum of energy, thinking that takes place as independently of our little I as possible, so that the action resulting from that active non-thinking can spring directly and spontaneously from total awareness, from the Void which is empty of the petty self. Non-thinking is a thought-process unencumbered by fixation or prejudice, which has learned to obey the impulses of our innermost being, the Transcendental Self. That only becomes possible, however, when constant practice has enabled us to acquire the ability to distinguish instinctively between the voice of our Self and the will or voice of our little I.

We thus attain what D. T. Suzuki has called 'motionless realisation' – an all-embracing mindfulness which does not cling to anything, an intuitive awareness and perception which remains unmoved yet looks deeply into our own being and at the same time grasps in a flash everything happening around us. When action arises out of such total awareness, it can be instantaneous since perception is no longer impeded by rational, discursive thought. Rational thought dissects reality; intuitive thought comprehends its innermost essence. Such thinking, which is essentially non-thinking since it contradicts all logic and rationality, surmounts the separation between subject and object artificially created by discursive thought and blocking access to the reality of things. Chuang-tzu says in that connection:

> Before conditions existed, *Tao* was. Before definitions existed, Speech was. Subjectively, we are conscious of certain delimitations . . . For the true Sage, beyond the limits of an external world, they exist, but are not recognised. By the true Sage, within the limits of an external world, they are recognised but are not assigned . . . The true Sage assigns, but does not justify by argument. And thus classifying he does not classify; arguing he does not argue. How can that be? The true Sage keeps his knowledge within him, while men in general set forth theirs in argument in order to convince one another. And therefore it is said that in argument he does not manifest himself . . . Therefore that knowledge which stops at what it does not know is the highest knowledge. Who knows the argument which can be argued without words, the Tao which does not declare itself as Tao? He who knows this may be said to be of God. To be able to pour in without making full, and pour out without making empty, in ignorance of the power by which such results are accomplished – this is accounted Light.[11]

For millennia our logical way of thinking has set up systems of thought, has time and again attacked those systems by means of other systems, and ultimately replaced the former by the latter, but to this day it has shown itself incapable of satisfying the spiritual needs within the very depths of our being. We have reached a point where we often assume that our life would be absolutely worthless without logical thought. Our soul is thus kept imprisoned in the conflict with itself. Instead of penetrating into tangible reality from the inside we are satisfied with bloodless notions about this reality.

Taoism, Buddhism, and particularly Zen start from the premiss that the highest reality of things, the highest truth, is to be found within ourselves, and that we can only know it through direct experience and intuition, not through learning, however 'convincing', or through some system, no matter how well-founded. The origins of Buddhism do not lie in philosophical knowledge but in the extraordinary vision experienced by a seeker after truth who found Enlightenment within himself after having scrutinised all the teachings of his time. He thereby proved that the highest reality is to be found in the innermost nature of human consciousness, not in the external world. If we wish to give credence to the occurrence of Enlightenment and the Buddha's subsequent appearance as unanimously recorded in the writings of all the early Buddhist schools, there can be no doubt that we are confronted with an experience of such all-embracing universality that all the limits of time and space, all individual limitations, were overcome in it. And thus the illusion of the materiality of the world of our senses and of the reality of an 'I' persisting in the face of this world was shattered.[12]

It is above all continuous practice, not continuous accumulation of knowledge, that leads to realisation of the Self and the highest reality of things. Even the teachings of Buddhism and Taoism can only act as fingers pointing towards the Great Truth. They are not the truth itself. That truth is carried within us and within all things, and has to be discovered and experienced by ourselves. Nevertheless, teachings and books can fulfil a very important function since they can communicate the truth to others, making easier their first steps towards the path and along the Way. They will, however, always remain provisional attempts and cannot claim to be in any sense definitive. At any rate their hinting at what every human being already carries within is often necessary and therefore of great value.

As we said previously, our normal rational thinking dissects reality, which in actual fact is a whole. If the archer were to apply that kind of thinking and to plan in advance all the individual movements involved in the act of shooting his bow, the whole process up to the discharge of the arrow would appear as something artificially constructed, lacking any inner flow. If that process originates in the archer's intellect, his shot remains superficial and can never flow from his inner centre. An archer who proceeds in that way has not even mastered the first step on the Way of the Bow. The correct form of the entire natural, flowing, law-directed process of discharging the arrow has not yet really become the archer's own if it has become caught up in discursive thought. Archer, bow, target, and shooting are still completely separate aspects. The archer has not yet experienced their fundamental unity, let alone being capable of bearing witness to it in his shooting. The artificiality of his intentional doing results in uncoordinated action. Undivided attention is still out of his reach. From one movement to the next, ever-changing anticipations are awakened by his thinking, preventing him from finding his own centre and emptiness through his shooting. He resembles the centipede which when asked about the secret involved in moving its countless legs so skilfully and faultlessly in complete harmony started to search for an explanation. Its legs instantaneously got into a terrible muddle and the creature was unable to take another step.

The spirit of the bow reveals itself to the archer in his tangible manipulation of the bow, and not in his rational thinking about it. In Kyūdō too it is accepted that all great things are experienced and created beyond the realm of thought. In archery non-thinking means to perceive from the inside the reality of the shot and the process leading up to it in unimpeded perfect mindfulness. That coincides to some extent with what we know as 'presence of mind'. Action cannot be adequately implemented through rational thinking. Such action would never take the whole situation into account, only fragmentary aspects. Shortly before and during the release of the arrow, even the layman will recognise whether an archer is shooting from the inside, from the fullness of his centre. If the archer is trying to rationally determine or even calculate how to 'catch' the right moment for releasing the arrow, there will often be a sudden, unmotivated, disconcerting trembling in his arms as he is holding the bow fully drawn. Because of his intentional and corrective thinking he will have lost balance and harmony between the action of pulling back the string and pushing the bow forwards, the harmony between the Yin and the

59

Yang aspects of the fully extended bow. He then tries desperately to re-establish that balance, but this is hopeless in most cases since any archer who relies on thought will try to resort to rational control. More often than not he will also lose the rhythm of his breathing, and with it almost inevitably the unity of the upper and lower parts of his body. That in turn will lead to a weakening of the centre of power and energy, the *tanden*. Such loss of strength in the *tanden* upsets the balance of the whole body so that even the firm position of the feet is threatened. The archer is then like a fish struggling helplessly on land, or the centipede which lost the rhythmic movement of its limbs because of too much well-intentioned thinking.

If thoughts connected with discharging the arrow arise during the preceding stages, they are usually directed towards conscious control or 'pre-planning' of one's posture – such as how to implement the next hand move or bodily motion. They may also be thoughts directed towards wanting to hit the target, thus originating in egocentric ambition. Since they are a reality, such thoughts cannot be deliberately driven away or suppressed. They would only become more firmly established in us if we tried. Attempting to hold on to them would, of course, be equally senseless. You simply have to acknowledge their existence and let them drift past. If you do not reinforce them, letting them be, they will decline in intensity. Unconscious concentration on our breathing and on what leads up to the release will make us invulnerable towards such thoughts. They can no longer exert any power over us. Then we can view them 'as dry leaves scattered by the wind of concentrated attention'.[13]

In his celebrated *Pi-yen-lu* (Jap. *Hekiganroku*) dating from the twelfth century, Chinese Zen master Yuan-wu aptly compared a person trapped in rational thought with a tub of lacquer. After some use that vessel will be covered with such a thick layer of lacquer that soon nothing will be seen any more of its original shape and the wood used in its construction. In the same way, the tenacious error of remaining caught up in rational thinking will cover up man's original pure nature.[14] D. T. Suzuki's proposition of 'I think it because I am it' rather than Descartes' pronouncement 'I think, therefore I am' should serve us as a guideline in the search for our true Self. That search is 'the search for the microcosm of the universe, for the image of the Tao in which all is reflected. It is not a search which demands that we become more than we are by nature, but a search in which we learn to acknowledge that we are more than we know.'[15]

Intentional thinking during the action of discharging an arrow is undeniably wrong. It goes without saying, however, that it is necessary to reflect about one's performance and to analyse one's mistakes after the training session. If possible that self-criticism should be undertaken in conjunction with meditation, perhaps in the posture of 'Sitting Zen', the meditational practice known as Za-zen. The archery pupil should also seek the advice of his master or more experienced bowmen if he is himself incapable of correcting his inner attitude or outer posture.

Let us once again consider another modality of the Tao, the *wu-wei*, the concept of without-doing or non-doing discussed in the chapter on breath and breathing. Like non-thinking, *wu-wei* is both means and end for the Way. We have seen that non-thinking has nothing to do with idle, vegetative, mindless dozing. Nor does non-doing involve lazy, passive idleness. Active non-doing usually manifests itself in spontaneous action which could be described as a kind of non-discriminating total awareness of creative intuition. Such action demonstrates that it is not initiated by the little ego of the person performing it but arises as our true Self unfolds out of our own primordial ground. An archer who acts in such a way has completely merged with the existing situation and its practical requirements. His action wells up spontaneously from his own Tao and the Tao of the cosmos.

An archer whose movements result from a mind which is as still as an ancient, tranquil pond will allow whatever has to be done to flow directly – without being consciously controlled – from his inner centre, his real Self. The manipulation of his bow is absolute doing, and in that sense he acts without doing. The charisma, refreshing individuality, and impressive sureness of true master archers ultimately derive from that capacity to rest absolutely within themselves, in their own primordial ground. They no longer act but allow the action to arise freely out of themselves. All their movements flow from what those movements demand of them. There is no longer the least gap between their true Self and the bow. Archer, bow, and target are one. Chuang-tzu says in Book XVIII:

> Perfect happiness and preservation of life are to be sought for only in inaction. Let us consider. Heaven does nothing; yet it is clear. Earth does nothing; yet it enjoys repose. From inaction of these two proceed all the modifications of things. How vast, how infinite is inaction, yet

without source! How infinite, how vast, yet without form.

The endless varieties of things around us all spring from inaction. Therefore it has been said: Heaven and earth do nothing, yet there is nothing which they do not accomplish! But among men, who can attain to inaction?[16]

An archer whose thoughts are non-thinking and whose actions are non-doing dwells steadfastly in non-being, in the fullness of his own emptiness. He does not have to chase busily after 'perfect happiness' and the 'preservation of life' any longer. Each arrow he discharges reveals that he has attained that state of being without having to make any great show of it. In loosing the shot he acts without doing, without deliberation, out of oneness with himself and the demands of the bow. He will also avoid any deliberate intervention, any desire to direct things, in his everyday life. He knows that such action is inevitably doomed to failure, remaining at best senselessly superficial. In both archery practice and his everyday existence he acts spontaneously without his little I.

Bushidō – The Way of the Warrior

This section will deal with Zen's influence on the warrior class in Japan. Such warriors' most 'holy' weapon was the sword, even though initially the bow was used much more frequently. That is why the bow as such will scarcely be mentioned here, but everything said about the Way of the Sword also applies to the bow and all the other martial arts.

Archery, the art of swordsmanship, and the other arts steeped in Taoist and Zen Buddhist ideas – from the Way of Tea to the Way of Writing – originated in ancient China, not in Japan. Only after the spirit of Chinese Taoism and Zen had permeated those martial and fine arts, which primarily served meditative purposes, did they finally reach Japan by way of Korea. Even Jūdō, the art of gentle self-defence, although officially created in Japan, has its spiritual roots in Chinese Taoism. In terms therefore of their spiritual background, none of these arts are Japanese in origin, but their cultivation, refinement, and above all their practical application are typically Japanese.

The term Bushidō is a compound made up of *bu* (combat, martial art), *shi* (warrior), and *dō* (Way). Bushidō therefore means the 'Way of the Warrior', which it must be conceded is a genuinely Japanese creation. Such a Way, which was the prerogative of the Samurai warrior caste, never existed in China. China did not have a caste system in the strict sense, and warriors were not highly regarded – in fact they were rather shunned and despised. In Japan, however, warriors headed the social hierarchy for centuries and controlled politics. Even today Japanese are proud of being able to trace their ancestry back to a Samurai clan.

The martial arts as a whole are called Budō in Japanese, and they are also known under that name in the West. Even though they were not originally part of Japanese culture, they became closely associated with the warrior caste and its Bushidō code of honour. Korean scholars emphasise that the character for *bu* (contest, martial art) originally had to be read – in accordance with Taoism and Zen – as *mu*, signifying emptiness. All forms of Budō would then be mudō-systems, 'Ways of Emptiness' or 'Ways to Emptiness' – and that expression would do full justice to their profoundly spiritual content.[1]

The term Bushidō seems only to have been coined in the early Tokugawa Period (1603–1868) when the martial art of Bushi (also *Buke:* warrior) no longer served during that long period of peace exclusively as a survival technique but was in danger of gradually degenerating into a kind of pastime. It was therefore considered necessary that the entire Bushi code of conduct be committed to writing. Characteristically, that age saw the publication of several works devoted to the ethics of the warrior class. Among them is a text by Yamago Sokō (1622–1685) who had close links with the Daimyō Kira centrally involved in the famous case of the '47 Rōnin', familiar to every Japanese child. The Rōnin (Samurai without a master) upheld the Confucian principle of absolute loyalty *(chū)* to their leader or leaders, particularly stressed in late Neo-Confucianism, pursuing that to extremes of revenge and ritual suicide *(seppuku* – also known colloquially as *harakiri,* disembowelment). In Japan that principle was united almost seamlessly with the Shintoist doctrines of religious veneration of country and emperor, thenceforth determining the Samurai code of honour.

The term Samurai is derived from *saburau* (serve, attend to). During the Heian Period (794–1192), the heyday of courtly culture in Japan, the collection of taxes was one of the most pressing political problems, resulting from battles against the Ainu, Japan's first inhabitants, and enormous increases in court expenses. During the ninth-century reign of Tennō (Emperor) Kammu, the subterranean storehouses in which goods collected as taxes were often kept had to be protected by special guards against rampant plundering. The Japanese warrior class gradually developed from these and other guards responsible for the safety of empresses, princes, and the high aristocracy, and also from the armies deployed against the Ainu. As the highest caste – farmers, craftsmen, and merchants were lower in the social hierarchy – warriors played a prominent part in Japan's destiny until the country opened its doors to the world in 1868. The spirit of this class is still to be felt in many spheres of life even today.

The two expressions Bushi (warrior) and Samurai (servant, attendant) were soon used as equivalent expressions for designation of the warrior class. The Samurai code of conduct, which was developed between the eighth and eleventh centuries and committed to writing in the seventeenth century, was very different from that of the other social classes, even though they too also emulated Bushidō ideals.

A Samurai's first task was, of course, to learn the martial arts, which originally meant the art of archery. Until the twelfth century the bow was used much more frequently in combat than the sword. Apart from his skill in those two disciplines, the Samurai also had to demonstrate mastery of the art of horsemanship and as a horse-archer. In addition he was expected to be thrifty, a character trait that was a matter of course for many of the lower Samurai. They often had to survive in abject poverty, not seldom as highwaymen and robbers, since physical labour and commerce were forbidden to them, and there were frequent redistributions of land, price increases, and considerable inflation.

The Samurai code of honour dictated consideration and justice, and also that the warrior should under no circumstances give expression to his feelings or allow himself any unacceptable form of behaviour. Love of women – unlike love between men – was frowned upon and considered a weakness. A Samurai would therefore avoid public contact with women, but that did not prevent him from making use of their services in brothels and tea-houses. In that respect, therefore, the Samurai differed markedly from his European counterpart, the medieval knight, upholder of highly stylised courtly love and veneration of women.

In the context of this book, the most significant virtue expected of a Samurai was equanimity in the face of death. In Buddhism (and particularly in Zen) he would find theoretical and religious teachings about all the virtues demanded of him. They also furnished him with the most promising practical means for realisation of his ideals. Up till that time, Zen and Taoism had never been linked with martial traditions. Chinese monks and Taoists strictly rejected all forms of violence and combat. Such things were at most tolerated as self-defence in cases of extreme emergency when it was permissible to save one's own life but not to kill the attacker. Japanese Buddhism, on the other hand, had always – with the exception of its Zen schools – been power-orientated, deploying mercenary armies of Samurai and monks. Only in the sixteenth century were those armies finally defeated by Oda Nobunaga and Toyotomi Hideyoshi. Although Zen monasteries were not involved in such degeneration, Japanese Zen lent considerable support to the warrior caste, even though it may not have actively initiated the process. It should not be forgotten that it was only thanks to Zen's links with the military government of the Kamakura Period that it managed to establish itself in Japan.

Japan has always been exclusively interested in the practical exploitation of all imported ideas. A system of thought has never been taken over in its entirety. The approach was always selective with adoption limited to those aspects considered useful and exploitable in practical terms. Those aspects were then modified and adapted to indigenous conditions in such a way that they could be utilised in the Japanese context without, however, radically calling into question the existing well-established order of things. Confucianism was thus not taken over as a whole either, but only those of its ideas which appeared beneficial and could be integrated relatively easily. Of particular importance were *chū* (loyalty) and *kō* (piety). *Kō* did not remain restricted to the Confucian relationship between children and parents, but was soon extended in Japan so as also to apply to the relations between 'above' and 'below'.

Japan confronts us with the paradox that two completely non-violent philosophical and religious movements, Taoism and Zen, were enthusiastically embraced by a social class whose quint-essential trade was homicide. That can be viewed as a kind of ruthless utilitarianism which judges everything primarily in terms of its practical utility and thus only accepts what promises exploitable success and actually delivers. That utilitarianism is still at work in all spheres of Japanese life and thought, and is especially conspicuous in business. Japanese successes in that area are at least partly due to this no-nonsense attitude towards technological ideas from the West.

It has been rightly pointed out that Japan had to 'recognise in Zen the metaphysics which it was itself lacking. Without that metaphysics Japanese psychology would resemble a relativistic system of attitudes, gestures, and ceremonies – apparently without much substance'.[2] The ancient Japanese Shintō could not really make up for that deficiency, mainly resulting from Confucian influences. Apart from a demand for purity, it could not offer the ruling Samurai class much more than a mystical nationalistic *raison d'être*. Zen – as a practical mysticism rooted in the here and now, in the absolute reality of the present moment – could provide Samurai with a spiritual foundation and underpinning for a life that could at any time bring confrontation with death. In addition Zen possessed the spiritual methods and techniques which could help the Samurai master this path, even when he had reached its earthly end at the moment of dying.

His upbringing and training taught him to deal out and also to receive death. The disciplines he had been trained in involved dying as much as killing. That resolute orientation towards death taught him seriousness and dignity combined with an instinctive certainty and agility rather than Confucian inflexibility.[3]

The first contact between Zen and Japan's warrior class was established by Eisai Zenji, formerly a monk in the politically powerful Tendai school of Buddhism. He made two journeys to China, looking for fresh inspiration in order to revive Japanese Buddhism which had started to stagnate. He found a new spiritual home in Chinese Zen, left the Tendai school, and brought Zen to Japan where he founded the first monastery of the Rinzai school at Hakata (Kyūshū). He also succeeded in founding the Kennin-ji Zen temple at a Kyōto dominated by the Tendai and Shingon schools of Buddhism which had become paralysed by complex ritual, political intrigues, and other externalities – but he could not really establish himself there.

He ultimately withdrew to Kamakura, a centre for the warrior class and seat of the Shōgun government from 1192 when Minamoto Yoritomo deprived the Tennō and his imperial house of political power. Thanks to the support of Shōgun Yoriie (in power from 1199 to 1203), Eisai was accepted in Kamakura relatively quickly. From then onwards, Zen began to gain undreamt-of influence on Japanese culture by way of the warrior class. During the Kamakura Period the Samurai were the main vehicle of Zen's permeation of Japanese thought, but even then Zen also influenced many spheres of art and literature relatively remote from the warriors. That process reached a peak during the succeeding Ashikaga or Muromachi Period (1333–1568), and the whole of Japanese culture was then virtually indistinguishable from Zen ideas.

Critics occasionally reproach Zen with being extremely vulnerable to misuse since it can relatively easily be employed by the most diverse of ideological and political movements for their own purposes. D. T. Suzuki, one of the most important pioneers of Zen in the West, maintained that Zen 'may be found wedded to anarchism or fascism, communism or democracy, atheism or idealism, or any political or economic dogmatism'.[4] If that had not been the case, Zen would have lost one of its most essential features, its absolute freedom, gained in part by its refusal to tie itself down to any fixed set of dogmas, any 'logical' system, with a canon of rigid concepts and guiding principles.

Zen remains open to everyone and everything, and cannot possibly be schematised. In that sense it is even revolutionary, anarchistic in a positive sense, since it does not hesitate to break all ideological and political chains. It offers *every* person an opportunity of realising him- or herself as a human being within the cosmic context. The psycho-physical abilities gained during that process can, of course, be put to use in any existential situation. Whether one is a warrior or an artist, or sympathises with this or that ideology, remains irrelevant – with the important proviso that one will never attain a higher stage on the Way of Zen so long as there still exists commitment to, and some form of dependence on, any group or movement. Zen merely helps us come to know ourselves in our deepest being as *human*. It strives towards a liberation that includes liberation from ideologies and philosophies of life. Although the Samurai who practised Zen as an archer or swordsman also learned to kill better, it was the fighter who remained alive without having released his arrow that counted as the true Zen warrior. There is, however, no denying that the abilities the warrior derived from Zen disciplines were employed for the destruction of life – and no Japanese Zen master has ever actively objected to that. On the other hand, no Zen master has ever encouraged killing either.

Chinese Taoism is different. Right from the start, it rejected any kind of violence, combat, and killing since such actions are in opposition to the Taoist principle of *wu-wei*. If somebody has to perform a purely outer action – that is to say, if that action is not rooted in the depths of the person's being – he has failed. Lao-tzu's Tao-te-ching explicitly warns against the use of weapons and advocates acting through *wu-wei:*

> Good weapons are instruments of fear; all creatures hate them.
> Therefore followers of Tao never use them.
> The wise man prefers the left.
> The man of war prefers the right.
>
> Weapons are instruments of fear; they are not a wise man's tools.
> He uses them only when he has no choice.
> Peace and quiet are dear to his heart;
> And victory no cause for rejoicing.
> If you rejoice in victory, then you delight in killing;
> If you delight in killing, you cannot fulfil yourself.
>
> On happy occasions precedence is given to the left,
> On sad occasions to the right.
> In the army the general stands on the left,
> The commander-in-chief on the right.
> This means that war is conducted like a funeral.
> When many people are being killed,
> They should be mourned in heartfelt sorrow.
> That is why a victory must be observed like a funeral.[5]

Thus even in the case of victory the man who bears the main responsibility is supposed to stand on the right as befitted all sad occasions. There is no reason for joy and exultation because he knows he has not succeeded in acting in accordance with the fundamental principles of the man of Tao.

> They [the wise men] do not quarrel,
> So no-one quarrels with them.[6]

The man of Tao conquers without quarrelling. Even when Taoists practised the martial arts, they never actively intervened in actual battle. Training in the handling of bow, sword, or other weapons was for them a method of meditation, a means on the Way of Tao, and not an instrument of survival. That is one of the main differences between Chinese Taoists and Zen Buddhists on the one hand, and the Japanese Zen warriors on the other. The former took the principle of *wu-wei* seriously; the latter used it consciously as a means of survival, intended to enable them to confront death coldly and unmoved by fear, and to die or survive in full awareness of emptiness. One fundamental reason why the principles of acting through non-doing and of such total emptiness did not really appeal to Chinese warriors derived from the lack of any highly stylised ethos in the form of a code of honour into which such principles could have been integrated. In addition, as already mentioned, warriors were generally avoided as a social group.

Japan's Samurai, on the other hand, had been developing their code of honour since the ninth century, and it had come under the influence of Zen from the Kamakura Period onwards. To some extent it is only thanks to Zen that this code of conduct became what we today know as Bushidō. It was only after the emphasis on actually killing one's opponent was no longer of importance in the Japanese tradition of the martial arts that these ways of combat (Budō) again became what they had always been in China: Ways to self-knowledge on the part of the adept. That process of transformation got under way considerably earlier in Kyūdō than in the realm of the sword with its extreme accretion of symbolism. Frequently quoted pronouncements such as 'The sword is the Samurai's soul' testify to a cult of the sword which only began to decline after the end of the Second World War – at least in its worst excesses, since the cult still survives in a more moderate form to this day. One must remember that the sword – unlike the bow – continued to be used in close combat even after the introduction of firearms by the Portuguese in the sixteenth century. As a weapon of war the bow became obsolete from the beginning of the seventeenth century if not earlier, and from then on was only used in sports, games, religious and popular ceremonies, and of course as a Way.

The ability to die and the ability to kill were particularly emphasised in a Samurai's upbringing and training. Down-to-earth Bushidō warriors were attracted to Zen because it rejected intellectual speculation, insisted on single-mindedness in thought and deed, was practical and matter-of-fact, and occasionally employed rough and tough training methods. The Zen notion that life and death are basically one and the same was, however, of particular significance for Samurai. That attitude, more than anything else, helped them to fight more effectively and to die an honourable death. Zen training enabled Samurai to escape cowardice and fear, the greatest disgrace that could befall them.

According to Zen, life and death cannot be considered separately. Death is based on life, and life on death. The one is contained in the other with each permeating and implying the other. It is futile for an archer or swordsman to waste thought on death and related questions. Such reflections make undivided attention, the prerequisite for all effective combat, impossible – or at least seriously impair it. Such thoughts would also demonstrate that the fighter is still totally dominated by his little I. Such clinging to the external I, which at this stage is still equated with one's personal life, often results in fear of death. From there it is only a short step to cowardice if the Samurai does not take refuge in equally despised panicky recklessness.

Hōjō Tokimune was the first Shōgun to base Samurai training methods more directly on Zen principles. Under his rule Japan successfully withstood the Mongol invasions of 1274 and 1281, albeit with considerable help from the typhoons which destroyed the Mongol fleet. Tokimune is said to have asked Zen master Bukkō Kokushi (Jap. *kokushi*, 'Teacher of the Nation') for clarification of the problem of cowardice. Their conversation ran as follows:

> *Tokimune:* The worst enemy of our life is cowardice, and how can I escape it?
> *Bukkō:* Cut off the source whence cowardice comes.
> *Tokimune:* Where does it come from?
> *Bukkō:* It comes from Tokimune himself.
> *Tokimune:* Above all things, cowardice is what I hate most, and how can it come out of myself?
> *Bukkō:* See how you feel when you throw overboard your cherished self known as Tokimune. I will see you again when you have done that.
> *Tokimune:* How can this be done?
> *Bukkō:* Shut out all your thoughts.
> *Tokimune:* How can my thoughts be shut out of consciousness?
> *Bukkō:* Sit cross-legged in meditation and see into the source of all your thoughts which you imagine as belonging to Tokimune.
> *Tokimune:* I have so much of worldly affairs to look after and it is difficult to find spare moments for meditation.
> *Bukkō:* Whatever worldly affairs you are engaged in, take them up as occasions for your inner reflection, and some day you will find out who this beloved Tokimune of yours is.[7]

Cowardice and fear originate in the little I. Only someone who has understood and experienced that can attain the stage which will lift him above life and death – provided he follows the necessary practice. Any everyday activity is an opportunity for such practice. Zen is rooted in the Here and Now. Since we are embedded in the workings of the cosmos, all fear of death becomes superfluous. Many people appear to be little more than bundles of fear and guilt, lacking any real *joie de vivre* – which is ultimately the outcome of ignorance of that interrelationship. All their lives they remain strangers on this earth. They feel as if they have been 'thrown' into this existence out of a darkness to which they will have to return after a ridiculously short period of time. A positive attitude to life presupposes an affirmation of death as well as the realisation that we are never 'born', never 'thrown' into this world, but exist through and in it for all eternity. Birth and death are nothing but particular manifestations of the one life which is without beginning and end, transmutations from one form of appearance to another. Every beginning can be regarded as an end, and every end as a beginning. Why, therefore, be afraid of death which, viewed in that light, loses all its terror and – like birth – is seen to be the most natural thing in the world?

A true Samurai – like anyone else who has attained that realisation – is free from all fear. He sees no point in desperately clinging to life, and is therefore immune from the danger of offending against his caste's highest commandment: never to show cowardice or fear. He is no longer troubled by the question of whether today or tomorrow might be the last day of his life. He is always ready for the end. He has recognised the wonderful unity of life and death in his deepest being, in his unconscious, and the limitations of superficial individuality, the source of fear and cowardice, have fallen away from him. Uesugi Kenshin (1530–1578), a Samurai and military commander during the war-torn sixteenth century, exhorted his retinue as follows:

> Those who cling to life die, and those who defy death live. The essential thing is the mind. Look into this mind and firmly take hold of it, and you will understand that there is something in you which is above birth-and-death and which is neither drowned in water nor burned by fire. I have myself gained an insight into this *samadhi* and know what I am telling you. Those who are reluctant to give up their lives and embrace death are not true warriors.[8]

The seventeenth-century *Hagakure*[9] tells of a simple Samurai who approached the great swordsman Tajima-no-kami and asked to be trained in his art. The master wanted to know who the Samurai's previous teacher had been. The Samurai answered that he understood absolutely nothing of swordsmanship. Tajima-no-kami felt he was being mocked since he could see quite clearly that the Samurai was already a master. The young Samurai then declared that his only form of practice had been to grapple for years with the problem of death, and the issue no longer troubled him. 'That is just what I mean!' exclaimed Tajima-no-kami since the ultimate secret of swordsmanship involves release from the thought of death. And he declared the young Samurai a master there and then.

The Samurai loves life just as much as any other human being, a fact which is often forgotten when people talk about those warriors' 'defiance of death'. The only difference is that their Zen training liberates them from any longer clinging to their individual little lives at all costs. Their understanding of the nature of a greater existence embracing nativity and mortality enabled them to rise above the question of life and death. Of course, attainment and realisation of this becoming one with the cosmos and its workings was not, and still is not, the unique privilege of the warrior. This oneness is alive in every human being, albeit often submerged. Potentially everyone can attain it. The Samurai was, however, professionally confronted with that particular question almost daily, and the incentive to get behind the interrelationship of life and death was more immediate and urgent for him than for most other people. Nevertheless only a small minority of warriors were capable of penetrating to the ultimate truth about life and death.

In the *Hagakure* there is much emphasis on the impossibility of achieving victory in combat so long as the focus is on one's own survival. Only when mental preoccupation with life and death has fallen away will one no longer be defeated by any opponent. The warrior was attracted to Zen just because of that practical efficiency which helped him safeguard his honour as a Samurai.

An archer who takes aim without thought about life or death is superior to one who has not yet reached that stage – if only because he can concentrate exclusively on his task of handling the bow. No thought of *wanting* to hit a target distracts him. His attention is undivided and directed solely onto his action, the demands of his weapon, and his adversary. Automatically, spontaneously, and instinctively, he will comply with the technical requirements of bowmanship. Nothing can come between him and such action, hampering the spontaneous flow of movements. His faculty of perception is not limited by his attention being deliberately directed, infringing on holistic perception. Deliberately organised perception focuses on individual fragments of a particular situation, ignoring others, and can therefore never grasp the situation as a whole. An archer who acts from out of his 'full emptiness' functions with undivided perception, and will hit the target without fail despite not giving the least thought to that. The secret lies in always resting firmly in oneself, independent of any kind of influence, without thought of the target, without ambition, completely free, unaffected by inner and outer circumstances – and simply discharging the arrow. Only *that* ability reveals the master. His sureness in hitting the target is solely due to his ability to attain that high level at any time.

The work of Lieh-tzu, a fourth-century BC Chinese Taoist philosopher and archer, contains an interesting description of what can happen when two archers of equal stature confront one another. Neither of the two combatants could wound the other since their arrows met half-way.[10]

Pure Zen, following Taoism, demanded that the Samurai should not use his weapons as instruments of murder but rather as a means on the path to self-knowledge, to his own emptiness. One day, during a journey by boat on Lake Biwa, master swordsman Tsukehara Bokuden (1490–1572) was challenged by a hot-headed Samurai. The master replied that his art consisted of neither defeating others nor being defeated by them, but in conquering without drawing his sword. The Samurai insisted on his challenge and Bokuden suggested they should fight on a small island so that the other passengers were not endangered. When the boat reached the island, the irascible Samurai immediately jumped ashore and drew his weapon. Bokuden handed his sword to the oarsman, suddenly took the oar away from him, and pushed the boat back out into the lake. 'That is victory without the sword,' he shouted to the bewildered Samurai thus stranded.

The Taoist principle of only using a weapon in a case of extreme emergency can be illustrated even more vividly in another anecdote about Bokuden. The master had three sons who, like him, had all trained in swordsmanship and had to demonstrate their proficiency. Bokuden sent them out of his room and then placed a cushion above the door curtain. The cushion was arranged in such a way that anybody entering the room would knock it down when raising the curtain. He called in his eldest son, who noticed the cushion even before entering, calmly took it down, and put it back where it had originally been. Bokuden again placed it above the curtain and sent for his second son. When the son touched the curtain the cushion fell, but, quick as a flash, he caught and replaced it. As the third son entered the cushion also fell, but he cut it in two with his sword even before it reached the floor. Bokuden rewarded his eldest son by presenting him with a beautiful sword, telling him that he had already learned a great deal on the Way of the Sword. He recommended that his second son should train more assiduously. And the third he reproved: 'You should never be allowed to carry a sword because you are a disgrace to your family'.

All fighting offends against the *wu-wei*, but Lao-tzu recommends that when a conflict cannot be avoided a form of non-doing should still be practised, since each of the three main Taoist virtues – mercy, moderation, and self-denial – would be endangered by an aggressive act.[11] The one who gives way will win by allowing his opponent's assault to fall flat in a void, so that the attacker's strength brings about his own downfall.

Another form of winning without fighting, but also without retreating or evading the enemy's blows, represents the highest and most effective attainment for a Samurai. Perfection of mental power and skill in combat, derived from the practice of meditation, is demonstrated in the 'real' fight without a weapon. That mental power can sometimes manifest itself as an apparently demonic force which is simply invincible. Probably the most fascinating example of that is to be found in a book by Zen master Taisen Deshimaru Rōshi.

A young Buddhist monk had to deliver an important letter but was stopped at the town boundary by a Samurai who had sworn to challenge the first hundred passers-by to close-combat. The Samurai had already defeated ninety-nine. The monk promised to return after having fulfilled his task. Before confronting the Samurai, he went to see his master who told him: 'You will indeed die. You don't have a hope, so you needn't be afraid of death. But I will teach you the best way of dying. Shut your eyes, raise your sword above your head, and wait. If you feel something cold on top of your head, that will be death. Only then drop your arms. That is all.'

With that advice from his master, the monk went to the contest.

He stepped in front of the Samurai, took his sword in both hands, lifted it high above his head, and waited – absolutely motionless in body and mind. That posture surprised the Samurai since his opponent's attitude reflected neither apprehension nor fear. Having become suspicious, he cautiously came closer. The monk remained completely still, remaining focused on the crown of his head. The Samurai tried to find a weak point but did not find the least chink in his adversary's concentration. He finally concluded that the monk must be a very great master of swordsmanship. Only the great masters stand ready to attack right from the beginning, and this one seemed as immovable as a rock – and with his eyes closed too. The monk waited and waited, focusing solely on the crown of his head. The Samurai got frightened and no longer dared attack. At last, bathed in sweat, he knelt down in front of the monk and asked him for instruction since he had never come across such a master.[12]

The power emanating from that monk, acquired through the discipline of Zen, paralysed the Samurai and made him realise that his art of killing was based on nothing but technical skill, albeit of a high degree. Such skill could not prevail when confronted by someone who could transcend technique through the materialised power of his mind. The monk's heart had become completely empty and free of all attachments. He had penetrated to his cosmically conditioned inner centre, and his mental power was no longer subject to any impediment. The monk's demonstration of harmonious energy from the source did not present any opening for the Samurai's blow.

A world like ours can scarcely be imagined without conflict and strife. Taoism and Zen have, however, indicated a way of contest without violence or bloodshed from which we could undoubtedly derive some benefit.

●

Kyūdō and Ceremony

Genuine Kyūdō involves very little in the way of ceremony in the sense of external formalities founded on tradition. A non-Japanese observer may nevertheless see something formal and ceremonial in the whole process leading up to discharging an arrow: in the way the archer steps forward to the shooting line, the entire sequence of movements, the harmonised simultaneity of motions when a group of archers are shooting together, and above all in the highly stylised formal perfection permeating the entire procedure.

In Kyūdō, however, as in the other Budō disciplines and such arts as the Way of Tea, any clinging to form and ceremony is considered an indication of pitiful limitation. Individual movements, steps, and manipulations may be formally established in all schools of archery, but someone who merely strives to fulfil such formal requirements inevitably gets bogged down in externalities and will never penetrate to the essential core of Kyūdō.

Today, however, a surprising over-valuation of ceremonial and formal aspects is often to be observed, even among Japanese Kyūdō archers. The reason is obvious enough. Having got caught up in purely technical aspects of the discipline, many archers will try to conceal lack of progress towards correct shooting – embracing mental and technical aspects as a whole, and mastering them as such – by striving to fulfil the prescribed ceremonial with emphatic zeal. Then after all that display they release their arrows and miss the target – a pitiful sight. Even a chance hit would not change anything but rather make the fortuitousness of such success more blatantly obvious and only confirm the archer in his self-deception.

Japan's great liking for meticulous observation of formality is of vital importance in a country consisting of a great diversity of social groups where the respect shown to an individual depends on his group's position in the social hierarchy and his status within that group. Japanese groups are relatively unified and cut off from the world outside. They can only function as long as extensive harmony prevails between all the groups in society. In order to safeguard that harmony, a formal framework is needed, and that is often incomprehensible for outsiders. The individual components, their structure, and combination are, however, known to each group member, and are regarded as an established consensus. When Japan began to import aspects of Confucian ethics from China in the fourth century, it acted in accordance with an unconditional pragmatism, enthusiastically adopting whatever agreed with, reaffirmed, and strengthened its own Shintoist tradition, and promised to provide that with a philosophical underpinning. Among those aspects, Confucian notions of the unity of nature and humanity, loyalty, and piety were of particular importance. What was new and unfamiliar, such as Chinese Court ceremonial with all its elaborate forms and rules, was also appealing, and became the model for Japanese court etiquette.[1]

Confucianism holds formality and rules in high esteem. There is also a tendency in the writings of Confucius towards excessive emphasis on external forms and thus on ceremonial. This does not constitute the essence of his philosophy, but it led in Japan to a separation between such externalities and their deeper content. Contrary to the spirit of Confucianism, the outer form was suddenly regarded as being more important than the foundation on which it is supposed to rest. Confucius himself wrote: 'The Master said: ". . . Nature outweighing art begets roughness; art outweighing nature begets pedantry. Art and nature well blent make a gentleman. . ."'[2] Here the ideal of a cultivated personality is the outcome of balanced interpenetration of elemental moral strength and aesthetic refinement. Where there is strength of character but lack of refinement, all the personality mani-festations will involve a degree of harshness and roughness. If, however, the inner content is sacrificed to one-sided aesthetic refinement, literary dandyism will be the characteristic outcome.

Form and content are still in complete harmony there, with one aspect remaining incomplete without the other, even though that seems to be a more mechanical balance, a weighing of form against content. The tendency to over-emphasise the formal aspect, even in Confucius himself, is confirmed in the 15th book of the Conversations:

> The Master said: 'What the mind has won will be lost again, unless love hold it fast. A mind to understand and love to hold fast, without dignity of bearing, will go unhonoured. A mind to understand, love to hold fast, and dignity of bearing are incomplete without courteous ways.'[3]

And elsewhere:

> . . . to aim always at harmony without regulating it by the rites simply because one knows only about harmony will not, in fact, work.[4]

One wonders what else is supposed to be regulated through form when harmony has already been achieved. After all, harmony can only mean that outer and inner aspects have attained equilibrium and complement one another. An emphasis on form as a means of regulating or strengthening such equilibrium would inevitably destroy the natural harmony and at best lead to a kind of 'complete artificiality'. Confucius says that archery involves practising elegance of movement and sureness of hand. There too, according to Confucius, what matters is avoidance of any show of passion, accompanied by politeness towards one's rival: 'There is no contention between gentlemen. The nearest to it is, perhaps, archery. In archery they bow and make way for one another as they go up, and on coming down they drink together. Even the way they contend is gentlemanly'.[5]

Of course, that does not directly involve the Way of the Bow, but it demonstrates the origins of emphasis on the formal and ceremonial often to be observed among Japanese archers today. Confucian belief in and dependence on form and Japanese pragmatism – which borrowed certain Confucian rules capable of helping the closed Japanese group maintain outward harmony through regulating interactions between its members – established close contact. That has endured to this day, and continues to guarantee smooth functioning within individual groups and also between groups. Only in exceptional cases can the Japanese rationally comprehend and analyse the degree to which they have been moulded by Confucian influences. European and American Japanologists, on the other hand, still find it hard to investigate this source of the Japanese character, and all too often it is simply ignored.[6]

Unlike Confucianism, Taoism regards everything formal as a mere externality without any significance in itself. It believes that any clinging to outer form prevents penetration to the core, to the essence. For the Taoist the appropriate form arises spontaneously whenever the individual's action and behaviour – which are bound to manifest in a certain way – obey the laws of cosmic order quite naturally, automatically, and unconsciously; that is to say, whenever they spring from man's real Self. Everything formal, imposed from the outside, will become rigid formalism. In that respect too, Taoism is the antithesis of Confucianism, which, among other things, imagined that the world could be ordered by precise adherence to form and scrupulous observance of ritual.

Zen therefore occupies an intermediate position as a result of its greater concern with practicalities. Formal and ceremonial aspects are observed relatively strictly in all the disciplines and martial arts influenced by Zen but must never be divorced from what constitutes their essence. Only the spirit not the letter, only the essence through which form comes into being, is to be grasped, experienced, and practised. To become free from formality and ceremonial, to seek and live what is central – that is the Way where form begins to acquire a deeper meaning and can bring us to detachment. It also goes without saying that the art of ceremonial in no way represents an impediment to development of the personality for anyone who is in full command of ceremony instead of being dominated by it.

The fixed rules concerning formalities and etiquette are not primarily intended as assistance towards the archer achieving a superficial perfection of aesthetic form. They are meant to help him in his striving for self-control and to foster his own creativity. The way he handles his bow is expressed formally in his manipulations and movements, but is not restricted to that. He far transcends such rules since forms can only serve as aids towards the realisation of inner meaning. Viewed in that light, they fulfil an immensely important role. By performing the prescribed movements in that spirit, the archer has liberated himself from all ceremonial and formal aspects, and acquired a rhythm which will bring forth something of genuine aesthetic quality and artistic perfection. The layman often sees that as superficial ceremony if he does not understand that the archer's strictly regulated – yet apparently relaxed and harmonious – movements are not an end in themselves. Their significance is purely functional, and they are also intended to manifest the spirit and essence of the Way of the Bow by means of a form subject to particular laws. The formal aspect thus helps the archer transcend dependence on externalities. In handling his bow he opens a path to unconditional freedom, to unity with the rhythms and laws of the universe. His movements have surmounted all artificiality and show, obeying nothing but his own inner rhythm through which the universe manifests itself.

If he lacked knowledge and mastery of the entire process leading up to the shot, the archer would not be able to handle his bow in a natural way or achieve unity and harmony between body, spiritual endeavour, and bow. If the archer deals with the formal and ceremonial aspects as a rigid sequence of mechanical motions, he will get stuck in conventionality. Manipulation of his bow will then remain a superficial mock fight against the target, which is ultimately nothing but a ludicrous scrap of paper.

The Japanese language has two equivalents for our word 'form':

kata and *katachi. Kata* is probably best translated as 'Gestalt' or outer form, while *chi* literally means 'blood' but also implies a person's mind or spirit. Only when the archer's training leads to unification of *kata* and *chi* in the form of *katachi*, and to manifestation of their unity, has his handling of the bow moved beyond all the apparent externalities of the ceremonial. By observing the formal rules he can now penetrate to the heart of the bow, to his own Self. In its deep seriousness and dedication to the Way of the Bow, his practice has acquired a religious quality. It is indeed genuine religious striving that impels him to use his bow as a means towards breaking the chains imposed on him by his little egotistical I and awakening to his true Self. Viewed from that standpoint, the original Latin term *caeremonia* is not too far off the mark with regard to the ceremonial aspect of archery since its root roughly means 'religious usage' in terms of the external signs and actions playing a part in religious ritual.

Spirit and Technique

It goes without saying that in Kyūdō technical mastery is also of prime importance. That principle is emphasised too in Eugen Herrigel's celebrated little book which has been translated into many languages.[1] Nevertheless, many of his readers gained the impression that the technical aspect of Kyūdō is something akin to a necessary evil, a matter of secondary importance, which may have to be attended to but will soon take care of itself, provided one does not get caught up in it and, above all, always practises in the 'right spirit'. Even though Herrigel focuses on the spiritual aspect of archery, he makes frequent – albeit largely indirect – reference to the fact that spirit and technique constitute an indissoluble unity and that there cannot therefore be such a thing as merely external training in technique. Both aspects are thus always a part of training.

In my opinion, however, Herrigel's book does not quite stand up to serious criticism in one central respect. What is at issue is the way Herrigel got involved in the art of archery in the first place. He started practising this art in order to attain deeper insight into Zen.[2] Any 'bowman' (Jap. *Kyūdōka, Kyūjin*) will confirm that Kyūdō is primarily concerned with comprehending the heart of the *bow*, and thus with penetrating to one's own heart, to one's own Self. Intellectual knowledge or deeper understanding of Zen is not a precondition for bowmanship. From the very beginning, active handling of the bow is in itself a kind of Zen, a form of meditation, whether the archer is explicitly conscious of that fact or not. The practice of Taoism and Zen may be of use to the archer but is not essential. Learning Kyūdō in order to penetrate more deeply into Zen also entails the danger that such purposefulness prevents attainment of 'full emptiness' and a high degree of unintentionality in shooting following the principles of *wu-wei*. Herrigel's path did, however, take him beyond such initial ambitions, and he finally dedicated himself fully to the Way of the Bow as such rather than as a mere means to a greater understanding of Zen. His achievement in attaining the fifth Dan (grade) in just four years, and the rest of his book, amply demonstrate that.

All the arts influenced by Taoism and Zen have in common the idea that every spiritual practice is also a physical one, and vice-versa. In every 'Way' spirit and body, knowledge and action, theory and practice always constitute an interdependent whole rather than being dualistically related. That notion is based on the understanding – essential in Taoism and even more so in Zen – that only by constant practice and training can we attain the Great Truth, the Tao, and knowledge of the true Self and its harmonious union with the rhythms and powers of the cosmos. For anybody who wants to pursue the Tao, the Way has to be something absolutely tangible. Only untiring practical adherence will bring us closer to the goal. It will never be revealed by mere intellectual speculation and abstraction but only through practical action accompanied by well-founded spiritual penetration of reality. This reality of the Tao is to be found in the concrete verities of our everyday existence, which ought not to give rise to metaphysical talk but should lead mind and body to the highest degree of all-embracing wakefulness and concentration, and therefore to hard practice. Mind, body, and technique thereby constitute an inseparable unity.

Just as a painter only becomes a painter when he deploys brush and paint, so too will the archer only really be such when he reaches for bow and arrow and starts using them. All mere theorising without practical reference to reality, to existence, which does not even try to understand life in a practical way, will inevitably remain unsatisfactory patchwork lacking real impact. True thinking is active reflection within a concrete situation. It demonstrates the psycho-physical wholeness of man, which Taoism and Zen take as their starting-point. There cannot be any idle, passive reflection which at the same time is real. Action and reflection are originally one.[3]

In books and conversations about Kyūdō one may come across the statement that hitting the target is not the essential thing. That does not, however, mean that you can be a good archer whether you hit the target or not. On the contrary. When the arrow misses the target, that is conclusive evidence that – at least at the moment of missing the mark – the archer is still miles from any technical, bodily, or spiritual mastery. In the opposite case, not every chance hit is proof that the archer has already attained the level of 'spiritual' bowmanship. That is clearly illustrated by the fact that archers are sometimes failed in assessments for the different levels of competence despite having hit the target – or rather nothing but the target.

Hitting the target is not therefore the ultimate objective in Kyūdō. It does, however, represent the archer's ultimate and highest opportunity for demonstrating – to himself and others in the tangible reality of the way he handles his bow – what stage he has reached on the path to self-knowledge. Western sports experts would say that the number of hits reveals to the archer his present level of performance – but that refers only to externally measurable achievement, not to inner attainment in the archer's struggle with his outer, egotistical I. For Japanese archery, hitting the target is in that respect an essential step on the way of return to one's Self. In order to fulfil that condition, the archer must learn to master the technique of discharging an arrow as perfectly as possible. It is by no means an incidental, rather tedious matter of secondary importance from which one needs to 'liberate' oneself as quickly as possible in order to advance to 'real' shooting. Inner emancipation from the technical aspect demands preliminary and complete mastery. Herrigel must be comprehended in that sense when, like any true master, he says: '. . . accordingly archery can in no circumstances mean accomplishing anything outwardly with bow and arrow, but only inwardly, with oneself'.[4]

From the very first moment of practising, the archer has to keep in mind that deliberately hitting the target is not the ultimate purpose, involving exclusive concentration on learning the necessary technique. What is at issue is the gaining of peace and self-mastery, and rediscovering his true, hitherto buried I in its relations with the rhythms and laws of the universe. He will not be able to approach that goal – in Kyūdō or any other discipline or martial art influenced by Taoism or Zen – without hard and persistent practical training, inclusive of technique. An archer who misses the target has failed at that moment. An archer who hits it only because of his technical skill is not yet on the Way of genuine Kyūdō either.

The Great Truth, the Tao, is all-embracing and does not exclude anything, not even knowledge. Nevertheless, constant practice directed towards the Tao is the essential, not knowledge. Tao and Zen have to be *experienced;* they can never be attained by mere *learning.* Of course the archer has to acquire theoretical knowledge about technical procedures up to the moment when he lowers his bow after having released the arrow. However, he needs to apply that knowledge in the moment, and thus prove it and himself. In the final analysis, that entails overcoming theory by practice, and to some extent also surmounting the world through fulfilment in activity rather than through withdrawal. Knowledge and action, theory and practice, are a unity; and practice is considered the ultimate touchstone of theory.

The body, through which knowledge and theory are expressed, has to become a fully controlled instrument which automatically obeys the energies at work in us. Under no circumstances must the body execute the movements leading up to discharge of the arrow as if it were an agent of the ego and its conscious will. The archer would otherwise at best attain a high degree of perfection, but his handling of bow and arrow would remain sport on a high level of purely outward mechanical skill. His bow would remain a simple instrument without its own inner substance. The spirit inherent in the bow *(yumi-no kokoro)* could not reveal itself and would remain buried – as would the archer's true Self. In the case of a genuine Kyūdōka, however, the technique will have transformed itself and become a form of manifestation of the Tao. The technical aspect continues to play an important part – that of matter through which the archer's spirit and his spiritual evolution find expression. He no longer practises the technique as such but directs training towards purification and maturation as a human being, and towards becoming free and empty for the Tao.

Training and practice in the context of Japanese Ways never concentrate solely on technique but always on the whole person. That is an essential difference between practice as comprehended by Westerners and by Japanese. For Westerners the significance and objective of training – in, say, Western or European archery –

mainly involve external performance or the number of hits. Japanese, on the other hand, are primarily concerned in a discipline like Kyūdō with their own inner evolution as human beings. No matter what activity man is engaged in, a certain amount of training will always be a precondition if he wishes to attain a degree of mastery. According to Western thinking, that level of mastery shows itself in an objectively determinable, measurable achievement. In European archery the archer has done well if he hits the target more frequently than his rivals. He has thereby demonstrated his superior skill, and the matter is settled until the next competition.

Taisen Deshimaru compares sporting activities of that kind to a dangerous toy which may increase the body's stamina but does not go beyond that to inner consciousness. He regards the combative spirit and physical strength thus developed as being negative. According to him, they encourage sportsmen to play at war like little children, thus demonstrating a wrong attitude towards life. At any rate, there is no wisdom to be found in them. Ambition and the aggressive tendency prevalent in many Western sports effectively prevent such activities making any contribution towards enhancement of personal existence and human maturation.[5] Wanting to win only strengthens the competitive spirit, which is based on, among other things, that very urge to measure one's strength and skill against others. A higher dimension of being and existence will hardly be attainable by such an athlete. He will remain imprisoned by his little I and the wish to come out on top when he faces a rival whom he will have to defeat through strength and skill in order to save and enhance his image and reputation.

The activities originally known as 'physical education', which over the course of history became today's sport, were still inspired by the idea that they were contributing to the general psycho-physical development of man.[6] Even there, however, the central concern was primarily to develop physical abilities, so that idea quickly lost its resonance, and emphasis on nothing but achievement took over. With that, commercial interests, which control sport today, increasingly predominated. Where sport is mainly concerned with peak performances – drilling people, thereby degraded as mere automata, for this purpose only – it entails numerous dangers of physical damage.[7]

If the Kyūdōka misses the target, he will not regret his performance being worse than another archer's. Without attributing much importance to his rival's score as far as his own practice is concerned, he will deduce from his unsuccessful shots the stage he has himself reached on the way of personal evolution.

The sure, apparently instinctive mastery of archery technique which Europeans so often admire is based on memorising and practising technique until it becomes completely automatic. By transcending technique, the archer enters the path of active non-doing in the Taoist sense. The technical requirements of discharging an arrow no longer call for his conscious attention. His attention has thus been liberated and transformed into intuitive awareness whose action is instinctively correct and accurate.

From the practical point of view, the degree of automatic behaviour and precise repetition of technical aspects is crucial if the tension between the archer and his object, the bow, is to be overcome. He is confronted with the task of having to do something which, as a beginner, he cannot carry out in a technically mature form. The Kyūdō archer overcomes that discrepancy between ability and task (the perfect release of an arrow) by learning to master and internalise the technical processes step by step through constant repetition. That constant repetition relates, however, to the whole process of discharging an arrow and not to individual movements taken out of context. If individual elements were to be practised in isolation, the overall course of shooting would be broken up into fragments and the unity of man and bow would become impossible.

Only when the archer has mastered the technical aspects to the last detail can he completely dissolve the tension between himself and his bow. Only then will it be possible in Kyūdō to resolve the dualism between subject and object; only then can archer, bow, and target merge into one harmonious whole. The following passage from Lieh-tzu illustrates that advanced stage of Kyūdō archery:

My body is in accord with my mind, my mind with my energies, my energies with my spirit, my spirit with Nothing. Whenever the minutest thing or the faintest sound affects me, whether it is far away beyond the eight borderlands, or close at hand between my eyebrows and eye-lashes, I am bound to know it. However, I do not know whether I perceive it with the seven holes in my head and my four limbs, or know it through my heart and belly and internal organs. It is simply self-knowledge.[8]

When the archer has achieved detachment combined with full and undivided wakefulness and openness towards every expression of all earthly and cosmic powers, he has reached the goal of Kyūdō. His bowmanship has transcended technique and theory. Nothing escapes his notice, and nothing can impair his all-embracing and undivided mindfulness. Spirit, man, and technique have returned to their original unity. The archer himself has become the technique, and the technique the archer. By having learned, step by step, to master the technique and its rules, he has gradually come to realise that what really counts is not the form of things but solely their essence. He has come to see how all things are an integral part of the cosmos. He has risen above appearances, and has thus liberated himself from his own external form, his little I, which he can now see and experience as something utterly ridiculous. He has freed himself from the externalities of technique and his ego through having penetrated beyond them, putting them to fruitful use as part of his Way.

The archer has attained that goal not by actively wanting to destroy any external obstacle but by actively penetrating and making it his own through incorporation in his path and his practice. That is what is involved in the frequent declaration that although technique, body, and spirit are closely related, it is ultimately always spirit (Jap. *shin*) which is the deciding factor – and not just in the martial arts. Spiritual attitude is thus the precondition for any correct technique. That is a valid assessment of the spiritual component, which is certainly not unknown in European thought. In our society, too, the principle holds good that the creation of all true works of art transcends purely technical abilities.

The spiritual aspect of practice is emphasised in order to make quite clear that training must not be exclusively concerned with theory, technique, and bodily skills, but that the objective of all 'external practice', i.e. of technique, must be the ultimate trans-cendence of all such external appearances. To conclude, let us turn once again to Lieh-tzu, the already quoted life-long archer and Taoist philosopher:

Lieh-tzu was demonstrating his archery to Po-hun Wu-jen. He drew the bow to the full and placed a bowl of water on his left forearm. After he released the arrow, he fitted a second arrow to the string, released it, and fitted a third while the first was still in flight. The whole time he was like a statue.

'This is the shooting in which you shoot,' said Po-hun Wu-jen. 'It is not the shooting in which you do not shoot. If I climb a high mountain with you, and tread a perilous cliff overlooking an abyss a thousand feet deep, will you be able to shoot?'

Then Po-hun Wu-jen did climb a high mountain and tread a perilous cliff overlooking an abyss a thousand feet deep. He walked backwards until half his foot hung over the edge, and bowed to Lieh-tzu to come forward. Lieh-tzu lay on his face with his sweat streaming down to his heels.

Po-hun Wu-jen said:

> 'The highest man
> Peers at the blue sky above him
> Measures the Yellow Spring [Hades] below him.
> Tossed and hurled to the Eight Corners,
> His spirit and his breathing do not change.

Now you tremble and would like to shut your eyes. Isn't there danger within you?'[9]

What a ridiculous sight Lieh-tzu with the bowl of water placed on his bow-arm ultimately presents compared with his master standing over the deadly abyss without revealing the slightest strain or deliberate striving after perfection. What prevented him from falling to a certain death was not his accomplished technique but the unshakeable power of his spirit, endowing him with absolute stillness and sureness. Perfect technique by itself is no more than a preliminary stage – albeit a relatively advanced one – to what lies beyond mere skill and the mere scoring of points: a preliminary stage to the Tao, to the true Self and the real significance of Kyūdō.[10]

PART III

THE PRACTICE
OF KYŪDŌ

THE PRACTICE OF KYŪDŌ

Preparations

Practised as a Way, archery requires hard, persistent, and preferably daily training, which can never be finally concluded regardless of the level the archer has attained. Like any serious practice whose aim is to penetrate beyond appearances to the essence of things and the meaning of life, the Way of the Bow can only be considered to have reached an end with the transmutation of the archer's earthly existence, that is to say with his death. That is not unfamiliar to Westerners either. We have only to think of all the artists, poets, and scholars who struggled to complete their work, often literally until their last breath.

In Western sport, however, we seldom encounter such an attitude since it is usually concerned with record performances or at least high achievements, which are for the most part only possible up to the age of forty. A price has to be paid for the one-sided emphasis on the body and technique.

Such an 'age-limit' is completely alien to Kyūdō. In fact, the older and more mature the archer, the more profound his penetration of the Way of the Bow is likely to be. The best archers, technically and spiritually, are usually older masters. The fact that as he gets older an archer uses a bow demanding less strength is unimportant because that in no way affects the quality of his shooting or the level hitherto attained on his Way.

During the first stage of training, when the archer still has to concentrate on individual movements and manipulations, he does not shoot at the actual target but at a bundle of straw (Jap. *makiwara*) placed about two metres away. The distance of two metres roughly corresponds to the length of a Japanese bow. The archer practises technique on this bundle of straw 'on dry land' as

91

it were. The intention is that he should become fully aware that shooting is not merely a matter of hitting or missing since even a beginner will have hardly any difficulty in hitting the bundle of straw. The development of any ambition is thus counteracted from the very start, simply by not giving the archer any object which could foster it. From the first training session, the master guides him on the way towards understanding that the greatest obstacle usually lies in the egotistical desire to score a hit, ultimately preventing him from really hitting the mark and advancing on the Way.

During training even the greatest master will not confront the actual target before having gone to the *makiwara*, which is usually set up along one of the hall's side-walls, and practise there for about ten minutes. That preliminary stage allows for 'warming up' and in particular for purification of mind and purging of all false ambition. Whenever an archer feels that his little I is asserting its ambition and interfering with his shooting, he will also immediately step back from the target and return to the bundle of straw for a few minutes. It is likewise obligatory to return to the *makiwara* for a moment after completing the daily training.

A communal period of Za-zen at the end of the training session is also obligatory. In Kyūdō that is observed either sitting on one's heels as in the traditional Taoist meditation, or in the Lotus position with crossed legs. There too the issue is the same. The archer tries to leave behind all feelings connected with success or failure, together with all related false ambition whose roots lie in having hit or missed the target. Any kind of self-satisfaction has to be controlled, including the tendency to cling to one's successes; failures have to be acknowledged as such without reacting emotionally; and both have to be taken for what they are: as a definite challenge to continue working on oneself and the demands of the bow.

Triumph and disappointment are thus seen to be relative, a natural and necessary pair of opposites, which are basically always one complete whole. There is also a Za-zen period lasting about fifteen minutes at the beginning of every daily training session even before the archer approaches the *makiwara*. That calms mind and body, bringing about a state of poised composure and leading the archer to inner stillness, to his own centre. It therefore serves the same purpose as Kyūdō itself: to cleanse the mind of all superficial interference and external dependence so that the cosmic energies can work freely within the archer. During that Za-zen correct breathing is of crucial importance – as is the case throughout the period of shooting practice. Such abdominal breathing is practised from the first day of training, and the archer has to try and maintain that kind of breathing at all times of day and night, regardless of whatever activity he may be engaged in. That is difficult to start with, but after four or five months the archer will breathe automatically in that way both during the day and while sleeping.

The pupil learns archery technique by watching a master or other experienced bowman and trying to copy what he has seen and understood. Such learning by imitation is called *minarai* in Japanese ('learning by seeing'). To this day, that has largely remained the foundation of all traditional Ways in Japanese sports and arts, which explains to some extent why Japanese sportsmen have had relatively little success in Western sports. There is only a minimal amount of theoretical instruction. That means that the archer can only come to grips with the technical aspects through endless practice, that is to say directly through bodily sensitivity rather than the roundabout way of the intellect. Such learning is therefore predominantly pragmatic and little influenced by theoretical thought. Traditional Ways were thus spared being swamped with theory. That is highlighted by the fact that even today traditional Japanese music is only taught at very few of the country's conservatories.

To begin with, the master does not try to discover anything in the archer, no special talent, no genius. He helps the pupil by getting him to make a start on the necessary movements and manipulations. The pupil practises the technical procedure by constantly trying and repeating what he has been shown until he has internalised it to a degree where it begins to manifest itself out of his own centre – automatically, without intention, completely on its own. Unlike Westerners, Japanese in no way regard such automation as a threat to personal values. Automation only serves their purpose of reducing to a minimum the activity and tension of the I and the will. A Way can thus be uncovered which will lead to the adept's deeper I and to the essence of what he is handling – and later to the nature of all things. Finally, his outer I will fall away of its own accord, and he will achieve harmony within himself and with his surroundings. In the Japanese view, that is an absolute precondition for the ultimate crystalization of a positive personality at peace with itself; and only then can man become freely and spontaneously creative.

Automation, with that aim in mind, in no way involves the truly mindless – because entirely mechanical – 'drill' in Western training of technique. In the West such drill is, for instance, largely responsible for Jūdō's degeneration into a senseless power-game superficially concerned with defeating one's opponent. The complex process of struggle is thereby artificially broken up into individual standard situations. Those individual, isolated fragments are then learned through 'training' until they have 'sunk in', and the recipient of the training has become a so-called expert in a few limited aspects of the sport. That is a far cry from that 'precision in repetition'[1] which characterises any real skill and has to remain sensitive to the least deviation, gradually leading – provided the practice succeeds in fostering mindfulness – to a creative kind of automation: creative because it does not get bogged down in mechanicalness but can instantaneously and spontaneously adapt the technical manipulations and movements to the situation at hand.

That is another reason why Kyūdō training starts with learning to shoot rather than with learning to hit the target. From the very beginning the pupil is made to understand that the individual manipulations and movements form a whole, a stream whose flow is unbroken, sure, and calm – and such understanding has to be converted into action. All that is learned through imitation, which can essentially be pursued without critical thought. The master thus gives hardly any hints or explanations as they tend to speak to the intellect. That method is, of course, not at all suitable for most areas of scientific research in the Western sense, at least not where independence and creativity are demanded of the scholar. Learning by imitation will probably seldom bring about outstanding scientific results when what is required is independent analytical thinking, thesis and antithesis, and the separation of subject and object.

The principle of imitation is, however, all the more effective in the domain of the Japanese martial arts and the other Ways since the intellect's analytical faculties are not of prime importance there. In fact, scientific analytical thinking would only hopelessly block the directly instinctive reaction demanded by such disciplines, a reaction which is based on all-embracing wakefulness and completely unintentional total awareness. The way to such spontaneous immediacy flowing from one's very centre is long, however. That is illustrated by an old Zen anecdote about swordsmanship, equally applicable to Kyūdō. It tells of a young man who wanted to learn the Way of the Sword from a great master. After having assured the master that he was ready to work hard, the young man finally enquired how long it would take to master the art. At least ten years, replied the master. That seemed rather long to the pupil, so he emphasised that he really wanted to work on himself day and night. In that case, the master answered firmly, he would need at least thirty years. The young man thereupon said that he wanted to summon up all his strength and devote every moment to the Way. If that was the case, it would probably take seventy years, the master remarked dryly.

The young man gave up asking any more questions and entrusted himself to the master. After three years when the pupil was not even allowed to hold a sword but merely had to prepare rice and to meditate, the master suddenly surprised him with a hard blow from behind with a wooden sword. Such surprise attacks were then repeated every day, sharpening the pupil's spontaneous attention. He gradually learned to avoid blows instinctively without the intervention of his will. After some time, his whole body had awoken to all-embracing and undivided attention and full consciousness, and his mind had been freed of all ambition. Mind and body had thus been sufficiently sensitised to every movement in his surroundings, so the real training could begin.

In former times about three years passed before development of the archer's psycho-physical attentiveness enabled him to handle the bow without deliberate volition. Only then was he allowed to step in front of the actual target *(mato)*. Today he is allowed to shoot at the target after the first three or four weeks. The process leading to at least partial detachment from external influences has not, however, been in any way shortened. That still usually takes a lifetime, which is understandable in view of the lack of systematic teaching about the spiritual content of the Way of the Bow. In acquiring the technical prerequisites through direct imitation, the pupil is furnished with a means which will help him to experience more easily and instantaneously what is essentially beyond words and teaching – the inner content of archery.

Even when a learner has more or less mastered that means, he still has to beware of taking the technique for the essence. The "teaching", that is to say the master's hints, are nothing but ciphers and signs to be decoded by the pupil himself. The master's instruction is only the finger pointing at the moon, not the moon itself. Little by little the pupil will acquire the ability to grasp the meaning of such signs and to experience that meaning through his practical dealings with the bow until one day he will himself suddenly push the door open from inside. From that moment he is free of all deliberately practised technique. He is also free of the master who has until then assisted him like a kind of Socratic midwife. The meaning of his actions had to be conceived by the pupil himself.

●

Hassetsu – *The Eight Stages leading to Release of the Arrow and Stepping Back from the Shooting Line*

In the old days there were a surprising number of schools (Jap. *ryū)* of Kyūdō, and the three main schools are still in existence today: *Heki-ryū, Ogasawara-ryū,* and *Honda-ryū.*

Although those schools differ with regard to specific movements and technical aspects, they agree in all major respects. Above all, the training in the three schools shares the same spiritual foundation and the same spiritual objective. Hence one school is, of course, as good as another, but it may be worth mentioning that the *Heki-ryū* differs from the two others in that it has reduced the entire process leading up to discharge of the arrow to what is really essential. Its movements and technique therefore manage almost completely without ceremonial. This school's archery practice particularly stands out for the fascinating naturalness and aesthetic simplicity of its technique and the various sequences of movements.

The author of this book is a member of the *Heki-ryū,* which is why that school's techniques will be explained here.

Hassetsu signifies 'Eight Stages' and denotes the individual movements and manipulations which lead to release of the arrow and the archer's stepping back from the shooting line. None of those motions, from the first to the last step, must ever be executed in isolation from one another or in a jerky fashion. They must form a completely harmonious, continuous whole, flowing smoothly into one another. The whole process has to resemble a broad river whose waters flow calmly but steadily towards their destination, overcoming any obstacle on the way. While its surface constantly glides towards the sea with apparently playful ease and cannot be stopped by anything, undreamt-of powers are at work in its mysterious depths. Similarly, the archer's actions outwardly appear to be flowing with perfect ease and instinctive sureness towards completion of the shot. His strength is, however, rooted in his 'depths', in the *hara* with the ocean of breath and the *tanden* at its centre. All the archer's movements up to the loose derive their strength from that source.

As long as a river-bed is still uneven, the surface of its waters will be irregular and turbulent, and so too will an archer's actions appear jerky and unsure as long as his psycho-physical profundity and clarity can still be disturbed by external obstacles. The archer has to be detached from himself, focusing solely on bow and arrow, but that concentration must be free from all deliberate purpose and all traces of ambition must fall away. The more completely the archer can achieve that, the more unimpeded the psychic and physical powers of his centre will be as they bring forth his action. Ultimately the shot will be released from within the *hara*. That may sound strange but in the last analysis a good archer shoots with his stomach.

Even though this chapter is devoted to archery's external techniques, those must always be seen in conjunction with the bowman's spiritual training and the spiritual values inherent in the Way of the Bow. It is therefore recommended that the reader should refer back to the chapters on 'Breath and Breathing' and 'The Way and the Ways' before starting on this one, and also return to them from time to time.

1. *Ashibumi* – The Stance

Before stepping forward to the shooting line (*sha-i*), the archer waits about three paces back at the preparatory position (*honza*). He grasps the arrows – usually two, in competitions sometimes four, and in normal training sessions often only one – by their heads with his right hand so that they will be hidden from sight by his thumb. His right hand rests all the while on his hip-bone. The left hand holds the bow with the bowstring pointing outwards and the upper tip of the bow about 10 cm. above the ground. The left hand also rests against the hip-bone. After having bowed in the direction of the target (*tachi-rei*), the archer takes the three steps forward towards the shooting line, lifting his left foot first. There

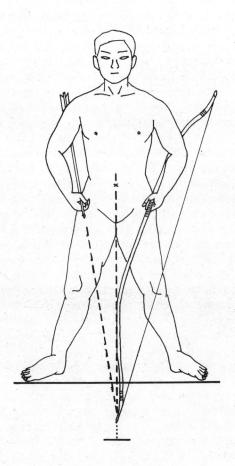

The Stance – the basic *ashibumi* position

The feet rest firmly on a line whose prolongation leads directly to the target. The entire body must be absolutely upright. The line through the navel runs vertically upwards into the sky and vertically downwards into the earth. This firm stance, free of all tension, must lead the archer to feel that he embodies a link between heaven and earth.

is deep meaning inherent in this reverence. It must not therefore be performed mechanically and without due care, but has to arise out of full concentration and inner mindfulness. By bowing to the target with that inner attitude, a crucially important inner relationship is established between the archer and the target (*mato*). The *tachi-rei* indicates that the archer is not interested in tearing the paper target to pieces with his arrows but views it as an aid on his way to self-knowledge, so that it is of importance to him. He communicates to the target that he will give of his best in the spirit of the Way of the Bow and his school's tradition in order to do justice to the target's status.

At the shooting line the archer then turns his left foot inwards, placing it at right angles to the right foot, while turning the latter outwards until the tips of the big toes form a straight line whose prolongation leads directly to the centre of the target. The two feet now form an angle of about 60 degrees. The distance between the tips of the big toes must approximately equal the length of an arrow (*yazuka*). The archer's eyes are not directed towards the target which is now to his left, but rest on an imaginary spot on the ground about 2 metres away. The upper tip of the bow is about 10 cm. above the ground on a line going vertically through the archer's navel. Extension of a line through the arrowhead meets that vertical at the upper tip of the bow. The archer's body is absolutely erect. The prolongation of a line through the backbone has to hit the ground at a right-angle and to go equally vertically up into the sky.

By regular abdominal breathing the archer deepens and stabilises the degree of inner peace and concentration he has attained during the preliminary meditation and his practice with the *makiwara* (the bundle of straw used at the beginning of the training session). He should try to maintain that inner poise and detachment from outer appearances as much as he can, even when he is not shooting. He should view his shooting as the highest manifestation to date of the stage he has attained on the Way of the Bow as a path to self-knowledge. The ultimate test does not, however, take place in the Kyūdō hall. The decisive touchstone is the archer's everyday existence.

He next puts the bow's lower tip on his left knee and moves the arrow (from the front) against the bow where the index finger of the left hand (*yunde*, bow-hand) can hold it in position. With two short movements the right hand now pushes the arrow forward in the direction of the target until it can be nocked (i.e. fitted on the bowstring). The bow-hand is now slightly turned outwards to the left while the right hand again comes to rest on the hip-bone. That posture is the basis for the next step.

2. *Dōzukuri* – Balance

Correct *dōzukuri* in conjunction with a good stance *(ashi bumi)* is the precondition for any satisfactory shot. If the *dōzukuri* is inadequate and carelessly executed, a successful shot will be impossible, even if all subsequent manipulations and movements come close to perfection. That would, however, be prevented by a faulty stance and poor balance since the following stages cannot be performed correctly if the *dōzukuri* is poor.

The body has to stand absolutely erect with the *tanden* constituting its centre of gravity and power, sustaining posture and the currents of energy within the body. Every movement, all concentration, all action and non-action, have to originate in the *hara* with the *tanden* as their source of energy. Only then can the entire body inclusive of all its parts act as a harmonious whole. Only then is it possible to focus spiritual awareness, which must under no circumstances be allowed to wander under the impact of distracting outer influences. All thoughts, whether about the shot itself or other irrelevances (such as spectators one would like to impress), have to be disregarded. Under no circumstances should the archer develop any ambition; this would constitute one of the greatest obstacles to a successful shot.

Body and mind have their centre in the lower abdomen. The Asian way of acting and thinking 'from the stomach' can only be attained and sustained through a naturally erect posture and calm abdominal breathing. The entire posture must be natural and unforced – in the same way as a heavy rock rests on the ground, immovable and unaffected by anything. Some masters say you should feel as if each foot were standing on a tiger's tail and you were trying to stop the animals from running away through nailing them to the ground by means of the downward-pressing psycho-physical energy concentrated in the *tanden*. The master often checks the pupil's quality of posture and balance by unexpectedly hitting the archer with his fist or an arrow, either in the stomach or from behind on the backbone. If such a blow causes the archer's body to move, his inner and outer attitudes are not perfect, and he would not even succeed in detaining a frightened little mouse beneath his feet.

The stability of the entire stance is sustained and strengthened both by psycho-physical concentration on the lower abdomen and the closely related abdominal breathing, and also by slightly tensing the thigh muscles and straightening the hip-joints in a natural manner.

The imaginary line connecting the two shoulders is parallel to that linking the hip-joints and to the *ashibumi* line between the feet.

The head is absolutely upright with the chin slightly pulled in towards the neck.

If possible the upper curve of the bow should be aligned with an imaginary vertical running through the navel.

The archer's eyes rest on a point on the ground approximately 2 metres away.

The correct inner and outer attitudes to be striven for in the *ashibumi* and *dōzukuri* stages are the essential precondition for every good shot. The difficulty lies in aligning the horizontals at the level of the shoulders, the hips, and the tips of the big toes, and in addition establishing a vertical connecting the upper curve of the bow, the nose, and navel whilst standing in a natural, completely relaxed posture, immovable and firm like a mighty tree rooted in the soil and towering up into the sky.

That posture cannot be attained by any effort of the will since such will-power would be centred in the head and thereby immediately prevent and destroy any balance. If you deliberately focus on a particular point, for instance the feet, the immediate outcome is that attention is withdrawn from another point, e.g. the shoulders, which then loses its balance. In that case conscious thought must move backwards and forwards from one point to another. The entire posture will be thrown out of balance because deliberate thinking is selective and unable to control the different parts of the body simultaneously. The centre of mind and body lies below the navel. That is illustrated purely externally by the fact that the middle of the vertical line between the bow's upper curve and the ground is to be found in the navel area.

Ever since the twelfth century, Japanese Samurai have in their own particular way emphasised the importance of that part of the body. Ritual suicide (*seppuku* or *harakiri* – disembowelment – in everyday speech) prescribed that that point had to be slit open by the sword. The stomach was viewed as the seat of soul and spirit, so the Samurai exposed his soul by cutting open the *hara*. In revealing his spirit, he atoned for his crime or demonstrated his innocence.

The correct posture of *dōzukuri* cannot be attained by deliberate control and correction but only by trying to achieve balance through first focusing on the abdomen, or more precisely on the lower abdomen. That is done by relying more on bodily sensation and instinct than on intellect. The archer must feel that the upper part of the body is resting calmly and securely on the abdomen while the *tanden* is being strengthened by abdominal breathing. The upper and lower parts of the body must never seem to be separate from each other. He becomes aware of a concentration of cosmic energies there, absorbed with the breathing, and can see with the 'stomach's spiritual eye' that mind and body are completely still, unmoved, and in harmony with one another. He can then be sure that inner and outer attitudes at least approximate to what is required. Beyond that there must be untiring practice and experimentation, best of all under the supervision of a master.

It is often difficult for a beginner to attain outer alignment of the previously mentioned parallels and the crucially important verticals. In that case one of the metre-high mirrors usually found in every Kyūdō training hall can be utilised. If the archer practises in front of such a mirror, he has to endeavour right from the start not only to stare into the mirror with his physical eyes but to look primarily with his inner eye, viewing the mirror as nothing but an important aid. The mirror can of course also be used in that way during all the other stages of *hassetsu*.

Before moving on from *dōzukuri* to the next stage, the archer consolidates his inner and outer equilibrium and posture with two or three breaths in preparation for the next step. His balanced posture must under no circumstances be altered during the entire process leading up to the release.

In some respects, an archer who fulfils *dōzukuri* to perfection, both inwardly and outwardly, can be compared with a monk in deep meditation. Of course, the archer is not seated but his efforts and aims correspond to those of the meditating monk. There is good reason for the greatest Kyūdō masters in ancient Japan also having been Zen masters. In both cases the abdomen, the 'ocean of breath', is the focus of attention; in both cases abdominal breathing is the means of attainment. For both archer and monk, the outer posture serves the inner attitude, and is at the same time

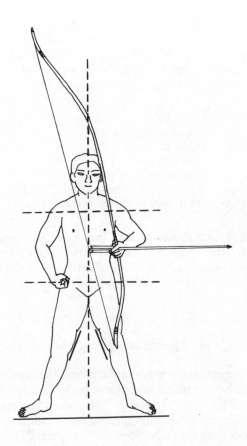

Dōzukuri – Balance and Concentration

The bow rests on the left knee. The lines of the feet, hips, arrow, and shoulders are parallel. The centre-line through the absolutely upright body leads vertically to heaven and earth. Any inner or outer tension would hinder that position. Through abdominal breathing concentrated on the *tanden*, the archer develops the energy and strength needed for the next steps. The centre-point for body and spirit lies in the *tanden* where the vertical through the body and the horizontal through the hips cross.

its external manifestation. Their objectives coincide too: steadfastness and absolute stillness of body and mind, becoming free and empty of egotism, ambition, and all other external influences, so that there can be harmony between the archer's or monk's inner state, his surroundings, and the cosmos. Cosmic energies can thus flow freely through man. He can deploy those energies, thereby experiencing himself as part of the universe and acting accordingly. Chuang-tzu described that state as follows:

> Body like dry bone,
> Mind like dead ashes;
> This is true knowledge,
> Not to strive after knowing the hence.
> In darkness, in obscurity,
> The mindless cannot plan –
> What manner of man is that?[1]

Desireless 'like dry bone' and impervious to any influence or distraction, the archer has focused his undivided full awareness solely on his task and his will is silent. That is the inner attitude which the archer should radiate at the end of his *dōzukuri*.

(●)

3. *Yugamae* – *Being Prepared*

During the previous stage, the *dōzukuri*, the main emphasis was on establishing a balance between body and mind, which also constituted the main difficulty. The succeeding stage involves a number of particularly complicated technical procedures. While trying to execute those manipulations as perfectly as possible, the archer must on no account interfere with the inner and outer attitude established at the end of the *dōzukuri* through now starting to concentrate entirely on the movements of the *yugamae* stage. If the archer were to attempt conscious control of those movements, his *dōzukuri* posture would immediately become forced or momentarily lost.

The *yugamae* also needs to be practised by focusing on the physical and spiritual centre, the *tanden*, without deliberation but with full and undivided concentration. The manipulations constituting the *yugamae* will then be initiated by the lower abdomen instead of arising in the hands themselves. Hands and arms are then only executing the impulses which – although coming from the brain – only find concrete expression in the lower abdomen. Once the archer has made those motions automatic to such an extent that they 'flow' from his inner centre without the deliberate participation of his will, the spectator will gain the impression that movements during the *yugamae* arise of their own accord and have a life of their own, taking its substance from the archer's centre. Bow, arrow, bow-hand, and shaft-hand will have merged into an inseparable whole. Overall the *yugamae* stage comprises three main procedures:

1. *Torikake.* Grasping the bowstring with the right hand and holding the arrow against it.
2. *Tenouchi.* Gripping the bow with the left hand.
3. *Monomi.* Viewing the mark.

Let us now look at these three main steps in more detail.

Torikake

With the bow resting on his left knee, the archer puts his right hand on the bowstring approximately 10 to 15 cm. below the arrow so that the string can engage the nock at the base of his shooting-glove's thumb. The longitudinal axis running through his thumb thereby forms a right-angle with the string and is parallel to the arrow. The right hand is then moved smoothly and steadily upwards along the string. The thumb should form a 'V' with the middle and index fingers until the arrow comes to rest lightly against the index finger about 10 mm. above the thumb. The archer tightens his grip by placing the first joint of the middle finger and then that of the index on top of the thumb (Thumb-lock). In that position the whole right hand is turned slightly inwards so that the index finger presses the arrow gently against the bowstring while the arrow in turn presses against the index finger.

The archer has to make sure that the longitudinal axis of his thumb remains parallel to the arrow – not only during the *yugamae* but until the *hanare*, the release. In addition, the right elbow must not be lowered, and all the muscles of both arms have to remain completely relaxed. Any tension in legs, arms, shoulders, neck, or hands would prevent the crucial inner and outer, spiritual and bodily, harmony which is the essence of Kyūdō, and a satisfactory shot would become impossible.

Torikake

The bowstring engages the nock at the base of the shooting-glove's thumb. The top of the index and middle fingers lie on the thumb. The arrow is held firmly on the bowstring through slight inward pressure from the right hand towards the body.

108

Tenouchi

Correct placing of the bow-hand (*yunde*) also presents considerable difficulties, even to experienced archers. When the *torikake* has been completed, the archer shifts bow and arrow across to the left until his right hand is approximately in front of the left side of his chest. That movement must not, however, affect the *ashibumi, dōzukuri,* or the *torikake,* leading to any change in the right hand's grasp of arrow and bowstring. The lower tip of the bow continues to rest on the left knee. As the bow-hand opens up, the index finger and thumb form a 'V'. The other fingers, straight but relaxed, are aligned with the index finger.

The right hand starts drawing the bowstring but only until a gentle tension is to be felt in the left hand. The archer then places the joint at the base of his left thumb firmly against the right edge of the grip whilst pressing the skin in the fork between thumb and index finger firmly against the bow from below. He then curls his little finger round the grip without it coming into touch with the back. The little finger has to be placed as close to the thumb as possible. After that the ring finger and then the middle finger come down between thumb and little finger – again without touching the back of the bow. There thus remains a hollow space between the four fingers and the back of the grip into which a pencil could easily be inserted. Next the archer places his thumb over the nail of his middle finger. Thumb, middle, ring, and little finger lie closely pressed together around the grip, but they hold the bow as lightly as possible. Under no circumstances must the thumb be bent downwards. That kind of grasp achieves the necessary firmness (as previously described) by the skin in the fork between thumb and index finger being pressed as strongly as possible against the belly of the bow. The nails of the middle, ring, and little fingers are in a straight line. Seen from the side, the thumb is placed at right-angles against the edge of the bow. It is up to the archer either to bend the index finger slightly or to keep it straight, pointing without strain towards the target. On no account, however, should the index finger curl around the grip. As during all other stages the shoulders have to form an absolutely straight line. At the end of the *tenouchi* the bow is still resting on the archer's left knee.

Monomi

With the lower tip still resting on his left knee, the archer draws the bow a little and turns it to the left until the arrow points in the

Tenouchi

Grasping the grip with the bow-hand. The thumb must not be bent, and under no circumstances should the index finger curl around the grip.

The *tenouchi* seen from the other side.

direction of the target and his right hand, which is holding the string and the arrow, comes to rest approximately in front of his navel. His torso, however, must not participate in this rotation to the left, but has to remain firmly and securely in the *dōzukuri* posture. The archer next turns his eyes towards the target. In doing so, his head and neck must be held absolutely vertical and under no circumstances be bent backwards or forwards. He is then looking directly over his left shoulder. Before settling on the target, his gaze rests briefly on the centre of the shaft and then moves slowly along its length directly to the centre of the target. His gaze remains calmly but resolutely fixed on the target until the entire process leading up to the release has been completed. That should not involve any rigidity of gaze.

The *monomi* is the last preparatory stage. While the archer's gaze is moving along the line of the arrow, ultimately encountering the target, he needs to check his breathing once again and, if necessary, regulate it. His psychic energy and inner, non-mental will-power have to be exclusively focused on the act of shooting.

The term *monomi* derives from *mono* (thing, object) and the root of the word *miru* (to see). If one were to translate *monomi* simply as 'aiming', that would not go beyond its superficial meaning. In Kyūdō *monomi* means something like 'penetrating the target with one's eyes' and not letting go any more – even before the bow has been raised and drawn for the shot. The expression *mikomi (miru,* to see; *komu,* to penetrate, fix) denotes the final stage of the *monomi.* That implies a degree of inner concentration on and absorption in the target which is not contained in our expression 'aiming at', referring more to the external physical-technical process.

Ultimately the Kyūdō archer should concentrate his gaze so steadily on the target and become so calmly and deeply absorbed in it that he actually cannot but hit it. After what has been said, it is hardly necessary to point out that from then on until the arrow has been released the archer's head must never move and his eyes never flicker, even if a mosquito is crawling around them – never blink or turn away from the target even for a fraction of a second.

Completion of the Yugamae

Yugamae means 'being prepared' with regard both to inner concentration and the external technical aspects. Mind, body, and technique each presuppose one another, and the quality of one is determined by that of the others. The spiritual attitude

Monomi

Completion of the *yugamae*. After the archer has concluded the *torikake* and the *tenouchi* he concentrates his gaze on the target without deviating until the arrow has been released.

nevertheless plays a comparatively more important part. It may not be able to completely eliminate any less serious faults in bodily posture and technique, but it can smooth them out to a certain – albeit minor – extent, provided the archer attains the additional inner concentration which is necessary for intuitive correction of any such faults so long as they are not elementary. In most cases, however, such intuitive adjustment cannot be repeated during the next shot. The archer then has to try and overcome any faults in posture and technique through initially deliberate practice.

In essence all three aspects are based on right breathing. Correct abdominal breathing is the foundation for all technical manipulations, and also of posture, spiritual attitude, and concentration. At the end of the *yugamae*, mind and breath have to be concentrated and substantialised to such an extent that *ki* (Chin. *ch'i*), the vital cosmic and psychic subtle energy won in this way, can be consciously directed into the centres of both feet, both knees, and the lower abdomen. Even though, when viewed from outside, only the upper part of the body is active during the *yugamae* (and in the subsequent stages), psychic and physical energy has to flow into the lower section and operate there. In that way the upper and lower parts of the body do not become two separate halves but remain a unity until the release has been completed. In addition, all the actions of the upper section of the archer's body – from the movements of hands and arms during the *torikake* and *tenouchi* to rotation of the head during the *monomi* – can thus be initiated by the spiritual and physical centre, the *hara* with the *tanden* as its central core.

4. *Uchiokoshi* – Raising the Bow

While the archer's eyes are 'holding on' to the target without wavering, he raises his bow with both hands until the arrow is about 5 cm. horizontally above his head, and the right hand, which is holding the arrow nocked on the bowstring, is about 10 cm. above the right eye. The impression should be of gently but steadily pushing a heavy mass of air upwards as hands and bow are raised. That can only be achieved by smoothly and unhurriedly raising the hands. The shoulders must not participate in that movement, but have to remain in the position parallel to hips and feet which they adopted during the *dōzukuri*. The archer will, of course, raise both hands simultaneously so that the arrow is practically parallel with the ground – as well as with the horizontals constituted by his shoulders, hips, and feet. Only the arrowhead is pointed fractionally downwards, just enough for a drop of water to run off it *(mizunagare)*.

As far as inner attitude is concerned, it is important that the bow be raised horizontally – steadily and without any unnatural psychic or physical effort. The archer, full of natural alertness and wide awake, must concentrate exclusively on the act of shooting without, however, deliberately exerting himself. Nothing must affect his concentration, even if the ground starts trembling beneath his feet. He stands firmly but without effort as if he were rooted in the ground, while raising his bow with an unhurried movement upwards 'towards the sky'. His spiritual and bodily subtle energy must never be exclusively directed towards a particular part of the body – especially not to the shoulders and chest. The subtle energy derived from cosmic sources through breathing must once again be concentrated or condensed in the *hara* with its *tanden* centre, and directed from there to the hips and the centres of the feet.

Before beginning with the *uchiokoshi*, the archer should have exhaled at the end of the *yugamae*, and then – as he is starting to raise the bow, he should again take a calm and deep breath. In other words, he should particularly fill his lower abdomen with air and thus with cosmic energy. During abdominal breathing the lungs are automatically supplied with air so the archer need not be at all concerned about them. If the lungs were filled with an excessive amount of air, there would be a danger of too much energy streaming into the upper section of the body. As a result the abdomen would lose its function as the centre of all psychic and physical action during the process of discharging an arrow. The energy centre would be displaced upwards and the upper half of the body would unsuccessfully attempt to act in isolation from the lower part. The archer's foothold would immediately be lost; the mental concentration originating in the centre would be destroyed; secure bodily posture and equilibrium would be shaken; the individual parts of the body would start acting independently of one another; and the psycho-physical and technical unity of the entire process leading up to the release would be shattered.

The archer starts to inhale again when raising the bow in such a way that the arrow always remains more or less horizontal in relation to the sky, his shoulders, hips, and the ground. This inhalation must totally coincide with the upward motion. From his very first training session the archer should endeavour to manage on the volume of air taken in with this breath until the arrow has been released. If possible, he should not inhale again from then on. That can only be done, however, if he concentrates all the energy absorbed with the last inhalation in the *tanden*, directing it from there mainly downwards into the legs and feet. Although the bow is being raised upwards, the energy is directed downwards – at least until the arrow has been discharged from the bowstring. Only in that way will the spiritual and physical centre be upheld, will the abdomen remain energised, until the loose – as a precondition for the arrow being shot 'from the abdomen'.

In order to attain that 'timing' in breathing, there is another recommendable method for when the archer has the feeling that the oxygen taken in during the *uchiokoshi* will not last until the release. In that case, while drawing the bow he exhales again by pressing the air downwards and outwards with assistance from the lower abdomen muscles, and starts to inhale once more when the bowstring is fully drawn. That method is as good as the first. Its disadvantage, especially for beginners, is that the process of energy concentration in the lower abdomen is interrupted or stopped, and has to begin again when the bow is drawn. That may, however, impair the equilibrium and unity of the upper and lower sections of the body just a short time before the loose. The archer should definitely inhale once more during the entire process of drawing his bow, thereby endeavouring to correct his inner and outer attitude, if that equilibrium, unity, and the associated sureness of physical and mental attitude have not been attained by completion of the *uchiokoshi*, or have been disturbed by outer influences or inner lack of concentration.

●

5. *Hikiwake* – The Draw

The action of drawing the bow will reveal – if that has not already happened – whether the archer is shooting 'from inside' or is merely employing external physical strength, technique, and will-power. Even though drawing demands a certain amount of strength, depending on the bow's draw weight, that strength must under no circumstances be derived solely from the arm muscles. It has to originate in the *tanden*. That is to say it has to flow from the abdomen upwards. If it were only generated in the arm muscles, the stability of posture attained in the *dōzukuri* would be lost, as would the unity of upper and lower body, and with it the archer's mental clarity and poise.

After the *uchiokoshi* the left hand pushes the bow forward towards the target, and the right hand begins to pull back the bowstring almost simultaneously. In reality the right hand does not itself perform that action. It only holds the arrow in place on the string and allows itself to be pulled backwards by the strength of the right elbow. The palm is slightly inclined downwards while the wrist remains almost straight.

The Japanese bow is thus not drawn just by pulling the string backwards but has to be simultaneously pushed forwards by the *yunde*, the bow-hand.

The pushing and pulling must not be forced but have to occur calmly and firmly so that the archer feels that the pushing is stronger than the pulling. The action of pushing and pulling coincide, so the arrow remains in an almost horizontal position in relation to the ground until it finally leaves the string. When the shaft feathers are approximately 10 cm. above the right eye, the right hand (or rather the right elbow) begins to draw the bowstring down until the shaft lightly touches the corner of the mouth *(hozuke)* and the front of the shaft feathers is just behind the mouth. While the right hand (elbow) is pulling the string down, the bow-hand is of course also lowered. Both hands are horizontally aligned until the arrow is released.

During the *hikiwake* (hiki, pull; *wakeru*, divide) the archer mainly has to direct attention to his shoulders. That must of course occur through inner alertness and without participation of his will. It is imperative that his shoulders are in a straight line. Under no circumstances should they be hunched or tensed upwards, which can easily happen as the right arm pulls the string backwards. Neither should the shoulders be moved sideways or one be higher than the other. That straight line can only be attained when the strength of the left arm, which is pushing the bow forwards, flows fully into the bow and does not get stuck in the left shoulder or left wrist. In addition the bowstring should not be drawn by the right hand or wrist. All the strength and energy required for that must be concentrated in the right elbow.

The energy needed for pushing the bow forward with the left arm (not the hand) must not be generated in the wrist or elbow but

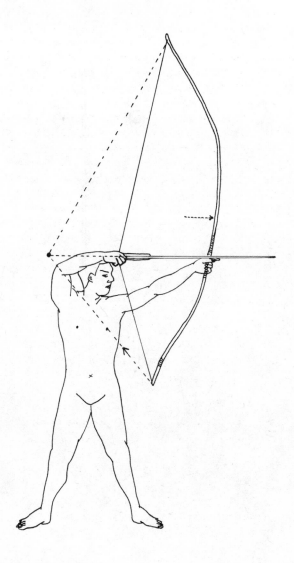

Hikiwake – The Draw (1)

The *uchiokoshi* has been completed and is followed by the *hikiwake*, the drawing of the bow. The left hand pushes the bow forward while the right hand, utilising the strength of the elbow, pulls the bowstring backwards. The *tanden* is the source and centre of the strength necessary for that action.

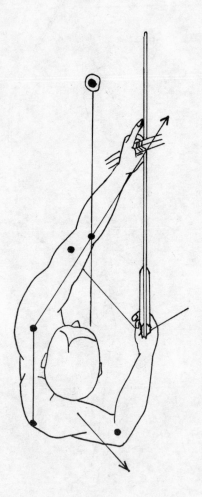

Hikiwake (2)

The start of the draw seen from above. A very high degree of attention must be devoted to the shoulders. It is absolutely necessary that they should be level and parallel to the line of the arrow. The archer's gaze runs across the inner side of the elbow directly to the target. The elbows are stretched. The arrows in the diagram indicate the direction of the energy flow during that stretching.

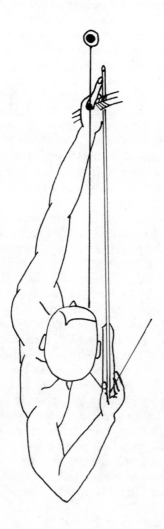

Hikiwake (3)

The stretching and pushing of the shoulders has almost reached the next stage, the *kai*. The shoulders and arrow-line are virtually parallel. The archer's gaze now runs through the base of the left index finger directly to the target.

has to come from the left shoulder. That is, however, only possible if the archer pushes his left shoulder down and slightly forward so that it rests firmly on his upper body, which in turn sits solidly on the lower part of the body. In that way the shoulders also come into contact with the *tanden* and can be supplied with energy from there. Mere muscular strength is therefore hardly necessary. Also of importance is the fact that the two shoulders thereby remain level and horizontal, provided the energy required for drawing the bow does not come from the right wrist. It must come from the right elbow. If the left wrist or left elbow supplied the energy for pushing and the right wrist for pulling, the two shoulders would not be even or in a straight line. The important balance *(tsuriai)* between the bow-arm and the right arm would thus be impeded or destroyed.

When the bow is fully drawn, the right hand will almost touch the shoulder. The arrow is then parallel to the line of the two shoulders, to that of the pelvis, and to the *ashibumi* line between the feet. The bowstring touches the chest, and the arrow rests lightly against the right cheek *(hozuke)*. The 'Balance of the Big Three' *(daisan-no tsuriai* – the unity of bow-hand, right hand, and right elbow) has been achieved. Other equivalent expressions are *sō-no osamari* ('The ultimate form of both sides') and *chichi-haha-no osamari*. *'Osamari'* roughly means 'to bring to completion' but also implies the aspect of success, so that it could also be translated as 'successful completion'. *'Sō'* simply means 'both' – that is to say, the left arm and the right arm. *'Chichi'* is the father and *'haha'* the mother. *Chichi-haha-no osamari* therefore designates a perfect relationship between father and mother (the male and the female principle) – a very apt metaphor for the harmony between the bow-arm and the right arm. In a poem about archery the hands are compared to the sun and the moon. That indicates the link with Taoism, which assigns the sun to Yang and the moon to Yin on whose harmonious interplay man's fortune and misfortune ultimately depend.

The ultimate foundation for this balance and harmony within the 'Big Three' is correct abdominal breathing. While the right arm (or rather elbow) pulls and the left arm (or rather shoulder) pushes, the archer keeps the air taken in during the *uchiokoshi* concentrated in the *tanden*. The further he draws the bow, the more he will press this air without any particular expenditure of effort down into the bottom of the lower abdomen where it is increasingly transformed into spiritual and physical energy. He will feel that by inhaling he has absorbed both air and an element of cosmic subtle energy, which then takes effect, calming the mind and making it indifferent to all distracting influences. It endows his posture with the firmness of a rock, so that his upper and lower body constitute a secure unity. His whole body, centred on the *tanden*, appears to be immovably rooted in the ground.

Once the *hikiwake* has reached completion, the archer has attained the following 'five crosses' as well as the previously mentioned parallels. These crosses are between:

1. the bow and the arrow;
2. the archery glove thumb and the string;
3. the bow-hand and the bow;
4. the backbone and the two shoulders;
5. the carotid artery and the arrow.

When the parallels and the five crosses have been attained, the drawing of the bow will be free of all unnatural effort and appear to be a completely smooth, harmonious process, whereby the bow, the arrow, the archer, and the macrocosmos in which their action takes place have merged into a truly perfect whole.

●

6. *Kai (Nobiai, Jiman)* – Holding at Full Draw: Final Stretching and Extending, the Final Concentration before the Release

This stage involves intensification of the previously attained bodily and psychic states, and no new movements will be performed. With completion of the *hikiwake* the process has almost reached its culmination in the *hanare*, the release of the arrow. Although it does not entail further activity, the *kai* plays a decisive part in the quality of the shot. 'Kai' in this connection roughly means to hit, reach, or 'encounter' exactly the right moment for the release. That suggests that this moment cannot be brought about by deliberate intention.

While the bow is held at full draw *(jiman)*, it is important that the harmonious unity of mind, body, and bow be maintained, and in particular that physical and spiritual energy be continually focused and exerted to the utmost degree *(yagoro)*. Only then can

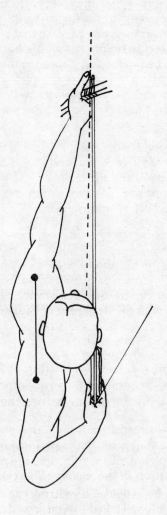

Kai (1)

The drawing of the bow *(hikiwake)* has been concluded. The arrow-shaft touches the right cheek. The archer's gaze runs directly from the left edge of the bow to the target – the right side of which is concealed by the bow.

the moment for the release be intuitively grasped. That final concentration will result in the arrow releasing itself almost 'of its own accord'. Once that maximum of psychic and physical tension has been attained, mind and body will react to it – naturally and independently of the will – by resolving the tension and releasing the arrow from the string. Alongside the psychic concentration that tension manifests in:

1. the pushing of the bow-hand;
2. the stretching of the right hand;
3. the left shoulder, which has to be absolutely level and stretched forwards;
4. the right shoulder, which has to be absolutely level and stretched backwards;
5. the chest, whose left side has to extend as far as possible to the left, and whose right side has to extend as far as possible to the right.

The final exertion in relation to those five points is also called *gobu-no tsume* in Kyūdō. Some masters refer to the ancient Taoist Yin-Yang system by calling the final stretch and pulling of the right hand together with the stretching of the right shoulder a Yin exertion, and the final pushing and stretching of the bow-hand and the left shoulder a Yang exertion.

The final expansion and stretching of the chest simultaneously to the right and left is called *nobi*. It must on no account alter the vertical position of the backbone.

The archer instinctively checks once again whether the 'Five Crosses' of the *hikiwake* stage have been attained, and especially whether the two shoulders are really level, one stretched as far forwards towards the target, the other as far backwards as possible without strain. Only when the archer's glove, or more precisely the upper part of the nock at the base of its thumb, feels the tension of the fully extended bowstring can the two shoulders be easily and naturally stretched forwards and backwards.

The spine and the neck are stretched vertically upwards as if the head wanted to push through the ceiling into the sky.

The feet maintain their natural firm stance on the ground. The line between the hip-joints is parallel to that between the two feet, between the shoulders, and to the arrow.

The *tanden* remains the centre of all strength and energy, particularly during this phase. When the accumulation of energy

125

in the lower abdomen has reached its peak, and the archer can feel a current of warmth (or rather a warm energy current) flowing into his two feet while the upper body sits comfortably and firmly on the lower part, he has attained the culmination of the process leading up to the release. Mind, body, and bow are one. The moment for releasing the arrow has come.

A few words about taking aim. During the *monomi* stage of the *yugamae*, the target was visible to the left of the left elbow, and during the *hikiwake*, to the left of the bow-hand. Correct aiming should depend more on the spiritual inner eye than on the physical eye. At that point the mind has to be as still as the surface of a tranquil pond which is as smooth as glass. The archer will then be in a position to take aim as if his eyes were fixed on a snowflake descending gently from the sky, without losing sight of it for even a brief moment until it touches the ground. The biological eye takes aim in support of the inner eye, and the archer feels as if he were illuminating the target with the energy of his bow.

From a purely technical point of view, the archer takes aim by looking with his right eye past the left edge of the bow. This edge conceals the right half of the target so that only the left section is visible. The archer can ignore that basic rule if, despite serious effort, he continues to miss the target when following the procedure described here. In that case he can take aim in such a way that the centre of the target is completely hidden by the bow. That method of aiming is called *yami* ('Eclipse', referring to the eclipse of both sun and moon). If that method does not help him hit the target either, the archer can try to take aim in such a way that the left edge of his bow only just touches the extreme right of the target, so that it is fully visible to the left of the bow's left edge. That method, which is only seldom used, is called *ariake* or 'Rising Moon'. It is hardly necessary to point out that errors in individual movements and especially deficiencies in unintentional concentration can never be compensated for by deliberately deviating from the normal method of aiming. The embarrassing outcome might be random hits.

Throughout the entire *kai*, deliberate thought should be reduced to a minimum and, in the case of more experienced archers, ultimately cease. The brain will intuitively – if possible without participation of the intellect – convey an impulse to the lower abdomen, directing it to initiate a particular movement. The lower abdomen then responds by materialising that impulse and initiating the movement in question. Even the final checking

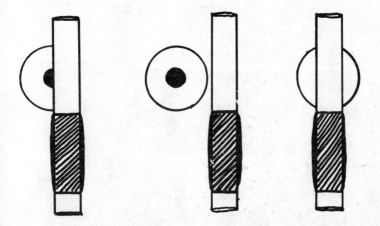

The three ways of taking aim:
1. 'Half Moon' – the most frequent form of aiming *(monomi)*. The right eye is directed above the grip onto the bow which thereby conceals exactly half the target. The left eye meanwhile gazes directly at the target.
2. 'Rising Moon' – where the entire target is visible to the right eye, just to the left of the bow *(ariake)*.
3. 'Eclipse' – The bow conceals the centre of the target for the right eye in the same way as the moon obscures the sun during an eclipse *(yami)*.

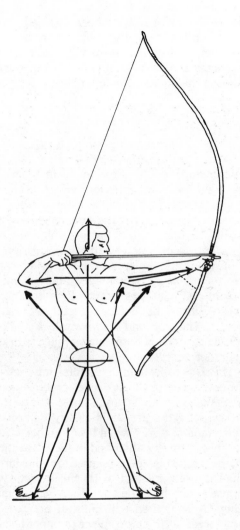

Kai (2)

The ultimate concentration of body and spirit before the arrow is
released. The archer awaits the moment when the arrow will leave the
bowstring as if of its own accord. His body is absolutely upright,
stretching into the heavens while firmly rooted in the ground. The
shoulder line is parallel to that of the arrow, crossing the vertical through
the body at right-angles. The arrows in the diagram indicate the flows of
energy and strength deriving from the *tanden*.

129

of whether the 'five crosses' have been attained – and especially whether the shoulders are really level – has to be directed by the *hara* and *tanden*. Just as it is primarily the inner eye that sees during the process of aiming, so it is the abdomen which does the 'thinking' during the *kai* and the other stages.

7. *Hanare* – The Release

All the previous stages culminate in the *hanare*. This climax arises spontaneously without any conscious effort on the archer's part when the spiritual and physical tension of the *kai* stage has reached its peak. The quality of the shot depends on the release of the arrow being as unintentional as possible. The release has to happen 'of its own accord' as the natural completion and outcome of all the previous movements and the psychic and physical concentration – just as an overripe fruit bursts and a bud opens when the right moment has come. It is the nature of their existence, not volition, that causes the fruit to burst open and the bud to blossom. The fruit and the flower lack volition. They are merely fulfilling the eternal cosmic law of nature thus manifesting itself through them.

That law is also at work in man, manifesting itself through him, and the ultimate purpose of all deeper practice is to regain lost harmony with that law and its functioning. The degree of concord hitherto attained by the archer is clearly demonstrated at the moment of the *hanare*. Only when his thoughts are empty, when mind and body are totally absorbed in the draw and taking aim; only when the archer is fully focused on the target, or more precisely has himself merged with the target, when he has liberated himself from his little I and thereby become open to his all-embracing I – only then will his shot be more than simply shooting at a target, a ridiculous piece of paper he is supposed to pierce. His shooting will then really have become a Way and part of the path to self-knowledge. The Way of the Bow will help him find his way back to the Great Unity, and the stage he has reached through practice to date can be gauged by the quality of his *hanare*.

The release of the arrow also gives rise to considerable technical difficulties. At the end of the *kai* stage the two shoulders have to remain absolutely level and must intensify forward pressure and

130

backward pull. The centre for the pull continues to be the right elbow and must never be the right wrist. Slowly and without interruption, the entire right forearm, including the hand, is rotated inwards towards the trunk until the point is reached (*hineri*) when the bowstring is suddenly released from the nock in the shooting-glove as the bow-hand pushes the bow forward. As a result the right hand flies back with great force but without intention, and remains in that position until the next stage, the *zanshin*. While the bow-hand is pushing the bow further forward and simultaneously downwards, it also has to push the bow fractionally to the left. That is necessary because the Japanese Kyūdō bow has no recessed arrow-pass on its right side. The arrow would therefore fly too far to the right if the bow were not turned slightly to the left.

All the different motions involved in the push and rotation, the *hineri* and the drawing of the right hand, have to be performed simultaneously in a completely balanced way without involvement of the archer's will. The initiative rests with the left hand throughout. There is no right moment for the *hanare* which could be learned through instruction. The archer's own practice and experience will have to teach him to grasp that intuitively according to circumstances. The following hints can therefore only provide a few clues but by no means get to the heart of the matter. That has to come to fruition in the archer himself. When the stretching, pushing, and pulling of the archer's chest, shoulders, and arms have attained full capacity, and eight- or nine-tenths of all the energy available to him is concentrated in the *tanden*, the archer's breath will seem to have acquired an almost mystical power and the strength of his muscles will appear to flow entirely into the bow itself. When the bow is drawn at that stage to the point where the arrowhead has been pulled almost back to its edge (*yazuka*), and the bow appears to have been transformed by the archer's energy and strength into as-it-were an animated object, the archer no longer has any alternative – and the moment of spontaneous release has arrived. A shot released out of that spiritual and bodily attitude will continue to resonate outwardly and inwardly like an unbroken silken thread.

The term *kai*, denoting the previous stage, was translated as 'encounter'. *Hanare* could be correspondingly rendered as 'leave-taking' or 'separation'. The arrow leaves the bowstring, and the psychic and physical tension which reached a climax shortly before the release is resolved. Any encounter in this world leads of necessity to a separation. One implies the other. One cannot be thought of without the other. Both aspects constitute a unity. That Taoist and Buddhist notion also finds striking expression in archery. The *hanare* is thus already contained in the *kai*. It has to be seen and realised as a natural consequence already inherent in the *kai*, and can be compared to a heavy dewdrop on a leaf which will quite naturally and out of necessity ultimately fall to the ground.

At the moment of the release the archer exhales, and he will have the feeling that he is imparting the energy thus released to the arrow as it travels towards the target. Some archers prefer to exhale only after the arrow has pierced the target. Both methods are equally valid. In all other forms of Budō it is generally held that body and mind attain the greatest concentration of strength and energy at the end of the exhalation. That is especially true of those forms of Budō where the main emphasis is on action and movement as, for instance, in Kendō and Karate. In Kyūdō, however, the rapid movements so characteristic of those martial arts are not of importance. Fully alert inner and outer composure and poise constitute the essence of archery. Some archers find it easier to maintain spontaneous full awareness, motionless steadfastness of physical posture, and psychic and bodily poise by way of the second method (exhalation after the *hanare*). Every archer has to establish through his own personal experience which of the two methods is better for him. It may be more difficult to remain motionless and firm at the end of the exhalation while the bow is fully drawn, and then to release the arrow, but experience shows that is ultimately the most successful method. To release the arrow during an inhalation would in any case be unnatural, contrary to all technical and spiritual requirements, and could not possibly lead to success.

8. *Zanshin* – Body and Mind after the Release

Zanshin delineates posture and state of mind after the arrow has left the bowstring. *Zan* means 'what remains' and *shin* can stand for 'body', 'posture', and 'form' as well as for 'heart' in the sense of 'spirit'.

At the moment when the arrow has left the string, the power of the rebounding bowstring causes the bow to rotate to the left so that the string hits the outside of the bow-arm – a phenomenon Japanese archers call *yugaeri* (the return of the bow). No shot is complete without that *yugaeri*. If the bow does not return, that indicates the archer gripped it too firmly during all the preceding stages, and in particular that he did not maintain the hollow space between his ring, middle, and little fingers and the back of the handle.

The archer remains in the position automatically reached after the *hanare*. He·does not change that position in the least. His eyes follow the arrow on its trajectory towards the target and he listens to the whirring sound of the bowstring until it gradually appears to fade away into infinite space. Only then does he relax inwardly and outwardly.

Although a good *hanare* indicates a powerful discharge of energy, a sudden release of extreme tension and concentration, the lower part of the archer's body remains completely motionless at the moment of the release and also afterwards during the *zanshin*. The *tanden*, the centre of body and mind which has been stabilised through correct abdominal breathing, absorbs the shock caused by the release, which among less-skilled beginners often shakes up the entire body, destroying physical and mental equilibrium and preventing harmonious *zanshin*. After a correct release, body and mind remain in a state of complete composure and concentration as if the archer had not even noticed the arrow flying off.

A *hanare* approaching perfection leaves the archer with a pleasantly refreshing feeling. His mind has gained a degree of clarity which – as any observer will notice – endows him with natural poise and dignity. As the shot continues to resonate within him, his expression is one of calm serenity. If his arrow has hit the mark, he will not rejoice. He will only feel that he has acted in harmony with the powers of the cosmos, completely unhampered by his egotistical I, and he will know that he is on the right way. Should he have missed the mark, that fact as such will not worry him much either. He will simply recognise where he is at the time and comprehend the defects revealed to him by the unsuccessful shot as an unmistakable invitation to analyse and then overcome them in further training of body and mind.

An experienced master can tell from the *zanshin* whether an archer has discharged the arrow out of the correct spiritual and bodily attitude or not. In order to do so the master need not even have seen whether the arrow pierced the target or not. This shows

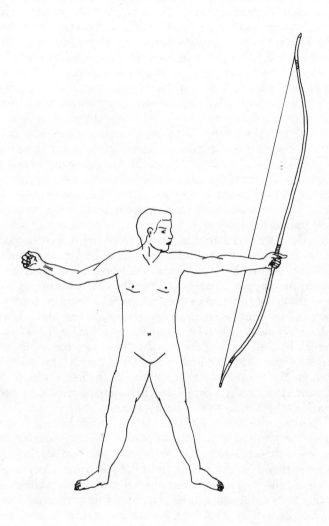

Zanshin

The arrow has left the bowstring. The rebounding bowstring has hit the outer side of the left arm *(yugaeri)*. The archer remains absolutely upright until the sound made by the bowstring and the shot's resonance within himself have gradually died away.

135

clearly that *hanare* and *zanshin* can never really be faked. It is embarrassing to see an archer trying to conceal deficiencies in his physical and mental attitude by an 'artificial' *zanshin* which does not derive directly from actions during the seven phases leading up to the release. That attempted suppression, embarrassing for any Kyūdōka or "Bowman", is found particularly frequently among archers who believe that their spiritual attitude is all that matters in archery so that correct posture and technique will develop of their own accord, provided one really devotes oneself to spiritual practice. Such spiritual practice, however, only appears to be spiritual since those initiates ignore the necessity of unity of mind, body, and technique. Their 'spiritual practice' is nothing but a romantic illusion concerned with appearances.

Once the arrow has reached the target and the low whirr of the bowstring has gradually died away, there follows the lowering of the bow, *yudaoshi*.

With a slow and measured motion, the archer simultaneously lowers the left hand, which is holding the bow, and his right hand, placing them against his hips so that the upper tip of the bow is once again held approximately 10 cm. above the ground. Only then does the archer take his eyes off the target by turning his head forward and looking again at an imaginary spot on the ground about 2 metres away. Then he places his feet side by side so that they return to their initial position shortly before the *ashibumi*. The circle is complete; the archer has come back to his starting position. He now makes a 90 degree turn to the left, looks at the target, which he is again facing, bows briefly to it, and takes three steps back to the *honza*, the preparatory line.

The *hanare*, the release of the arrow, thus by no means concludes the process. If the archer started to exhale during the *hanare*, he will sustain that slow even exhalation during the *zanshin* and then hold his breath until the *yudaoshi*. Only when his bow hand and staff hand have returned to the hips and his head is pointing forward again will he start to inhale and exhale once more. Only after that exhalation are the feet put together again. The archer faces the target and then takes three steps back to the *honza*. If he did not exhale during the *hanare*, the air is allowed to escape only after the *monomi* has been terminated – that is to say, when the gaze has again come to rest on the ground 2 metres away. The archer finally returns to the *honza* after inhaling once again.

While implementing these eight stages the archer must always be inwardly aware of the fact that each phase contains the one that follows, and that each consecutive stage continues to incorporate all the preceding ones, so that the individual movements, manipulations, and phases of concentration imply one another and could not possibly exist in isolation from one another. If the archer has fulfilled that primary condition, the action involved in shooting his bow will resemble the continuous, uninterrupted flow of a wide river which is steadily heading towards its destination and cannot be diverted by anything.

Eastern Practices for Westerners?

There is a prejudice, to be encountered on all sides even today, which maintains that Westerners are unsuited for Eastern methods leading to self-knowledge and harmonisation of the self with the rhythm of the universe, while Eastern man is said to be predestined for such ways. Both views are equally wrong and unfounded.

It is true that East and West are different and are based on different cultural foundations. That, however, only means that they are dissimilar, not that they are opposed to one another, let alone exclude one another. It will never be a matter of choice between or decision in favour of either West or East, an either/or, never a matter of hostile conflict in which one side tries to force its 'blessings' on the other.

East and West: strictly speaking, it is, of course, inadmissible to employ those terms summarily since both contain endless nuances and differentiations. Besides they are only the poles of an integral whole, poles that belong together like yes and no, light and dark, good and evil, like the restful Yin and the active Yang. They presuppose one another and already contain the individual elements of their complementary pole within themselves. The prejudices stem from reciprocal ignorance of this relationship and from the fact that neither pole has as yet felt or experienced comprehension of the other within itself. That deficiency leads to over-emphasis on what is peculiar to itself, which is then all too often set up as an absolute. That is one of the roots of Western arrogance towards the East. The same can be said of the conviction, particularly often encountered in Japan, that one represents something very special of which the West can at best scratch the surface. Any foreigner living in Japan rather than visiting the country as a tourist – in which role he does not threaten the Japanese self-image of being special and unfathomable – is reminded almost daily of the supposed inscrutability of the Japanese character. That particularly happens if he or she has a command of the country's language and is involved in what the Japanese consider to be 'quintessentially Japanese' matters such as the Way of Tea, the Way of the Flower, or Kyūdō. The Japanese often repress the fact that Japan's spiritual foundations largely derive from the Chinese mainland as mediated by Korea.

That is paralleled in the West even today by belief in the absolute superiority of Western thinking as compared with Asia's supposedly passive mental attitudes. The successes which have raised some Asian countries to the supposed heights of Western civilisation are often still attributed to Asian skill in copying and imitating, an explanation which does not undermine but rather accentuates the West's belief in its superiority.[1]

The truism about the world becoming smaller need not necessarily be a platitude. That merely points to the fact that civilisation in the technically highly developed countries in East and West has become one and the same in the course of their industrialisation. Today Europe is no longer 'Christian' as China and Japan are no longer 'Taoist' or 'Buddhist'. 'An inner logic implicit in the universal scientific process of subjecting the entire realm of public life to technical norms'[2] may have resulted in a superficial way of looking at things leading to the question of whether China and Japan can still be regarded as part of the 'East'. 'Europe is no longer European in the old sense, and similarly the East is no longer oriental.'[3]

We can no longer neatly separate the two poles by resorting to a few convenient clichés. Karl Löwith, the philosopher quoted above, goes even further. According to him, Europe is only now becoming integrated into the East while in the West itself it is increasingly declining in significance. However, Löwith also says that, despite the spread of technological uniformity and the internationalisation of technical know-how, the cultures continue to differ 'even though the Gothic cathedrals of Europe and the Buddhist temples of Japan no longer dominate the everyday existence of the masses.'[4]

The differences between Eastern and Western ways of thinking continue to exist. In that respect the world has not shrunk at all.

There are now, however, many more opportunities for studying and experiencing those differences in real life, and for trying to come to terms with them. As a result the West has a better chance of recognising, without great outward expenditure of energy, what Eastern elements it carries within itself. The East, for its part, can rediscover in the West certain aspects characteristic of its own culture. More than ever before, both poles are today given an opportunity for productive interchange, and with that the equally important chance of gaining deeper insight into themselves. Only someone who learns about what is unfamiliar, discovering that some of its aspects are to be found within himself, will be really capable of penetrating to the hidden depths of his own being.

Zen master Mumon Yamada, one of the first Zen priests to accept foreign pupils in his monastery, was once asked why he took so much trouble with foreigners. His reply was that he did not see a great future for genuine Zen in Japan, where external formalities and increasing exclusivity had divorced Zen from its essence to a considerably greater extent than many Japanese, including monks, were ready to admit to themselves. He was trying to transplant Zen abroad so that it might flourish there, relatively unimpeded by the limits imposed by tradition. After having shed all superfluous ballast it could then return to Japan. Daisetsu Teitaro Suzuki, the highly acclaimed and world-famous scholar and protagonist of Eastern thought in the West who spent a large part of his life teaching in the USA, held similar views.[5] It would be exaggerated but essentially true to maintain with Suzuki that what is typically Japanese about the Chinese–Japanese Ways is the emphasis on outer form which has by now been carried to extremes in Japan. In Budō sports there is also an increasing emphasis on results. In Kyūdō that means that achievement is judged in terms of the number of hits. When asked whether foreigners were at all capable of understanding the profundities of something as subtly Japanese as the Way of Tea, Sen Soshitsu, the fifteenth head of the Urasenke Tea School who had already helped numerous Europeans and Americans to attain one of the various degrees of mastery in that discipline, answered that Non-Japanese were not faced with any greater difficulties. On the contrary. He had observed that his Japanese pupils tended to get stuck in mere formalities far more frequently than non-Japanese initiates.[6]

Similarly many masters of the bow stress the seriousness and diligence of the majority of their non-Japanese pupils, complaining about the over-emphasis on technique and results among many Japanese archers who are often no longer capable of comprehending older texts which treat spirit and technique as being equal. That development is encouraged by the many competitions in which only the number of hits counts.

Some of the greatest and most renowned masters representing the various Japanese 'Ways' share such views. Scepticism towards non-Japanese pupils is usually only encountered at the lower levels, especially among those Japanese who by now only have a very superficial hearsay knowledge of their own culture.

We said previously that East and West are two poles of an integral whole, complementing one another and containing elements of the other within themselves. The essential thing is to cultivate and reactivate those elements. What is written and said about the incompatibility of those two poles results from the idea that differences and opposites are directed *against* one another, as if light and dark, or soft and hard, were antagonistic principles. If the West were to devote more attention to the notion of the unity of all opposites, if it were to subject to critical reappraisal its view of the individual as an independent 'I' confronting nature, moving beyond comprehending life as a fight against death, and, above all, if Western consciousness were to become open to experiencing the oneness of man, universe, and the Source of All Being or God, then our chances of overcoming many of our present crises would be reasonably good.

The 'ancient' Orient puts more emphasis than the West on such ideas, so it makes very good sense to study those concepts more comprehensively. A start was made long ago. In any case, the notion of the unity of all opposites has been implicit in Western thought from the very beginning. Heraclitus, the Pythagoreans, Plotinus, Meister Eckhart, Jakob Boehme, Angelus Silesius, Goethe, Hermann Hesse, and Albert Einstein may serve as the most prominent exemplars. Their views – so far as they correspond to those of the Asian sages – may never have become a force capable of determining the development of our culture, but they have time and again re-emerged more strongly during periods of crisis.

Traditional oriental thinking and the Eastern attitude to life does, however, also entail a great danger. Since oriental man tends to put too much emphasis on the inner Way, he all too easily comes to grief when life confronts him with concrete decisions which might call his frame of reference into question. Demands for adaptation to new ways of living and thinking are not easily accepted because of that basic attitude. While the West neglects the need to look inwards, the East devotes too little attention to looking out into the world.

In their attempts at surmounting today's crises, the modern Orient and Occident have to start from the roots of their own cultures. Any mere transfer of practices and methods would be nothing but empty imitation because the spiritual evolution of the two poles has been different and has created particular conditions which would militate against any fruitful, straightforward adoption of such practices. Our Western way has to begin with our Western reality. Western man needs to fathom and reassimilate his own culture. He will discover useful elements in the Eastern Ways which will be of assistance in that endeavour. The West must develop its own 'Yoga' as C. G. Jung suggested. In the context of archery this means that the Kyūdō archer must first recognise achievement orientation, involving the greatest possible number of hits, as providing one of the foundations of his cultural homeland. That must, however, then be transformed through practice of Kyūdō into an achievement that flows directly from his centre without any deliberate involvement of will-power. He has to learn about shooting, not about hitting the target. He will then hit the mark instinctively and with greater sureness than before. Many Eastern concepts and the means of their realisation are also to be found in our culture, so we can revive those elements with assistance from Eastern ideas and practices, allowing them to bear fruit within ourselves.

One of those methods is meditation – in whatever form, with or without bow. As contemplation it has always been known to us. If such meditation is practised for its own sake without any intentionally determined aim, our belief in the existence of an individual I confronted by the universe will gradually fall away as we return to our Self. That will happen as gently and unresistingly as a leaf detaches itself from a branch in autumn. We shake off the chains of our I with its desires and cravings. The opposites return to the unity of the whole. The meditator experiences a deep inner calm which makes him immune to the externalities of his everyday life – and yet he will not resist them. The return to the Source provides him with the energy for dealing with his daily tasks. In addition, by surmounting the world of appearances within himself he gains a wonderful freedom which will exert an outer impact by example alone, thus helping open other people's eyes. Hence the meditator, with or without a bow, will be working

141

towards general transformation. Such transformation will essentially bring about transcendence of the notion that we have been thrown *into* the world. The dualities of man and nature, man and his fellow man, will thus have been overcome.[7] The meditator and others will regain the knowledge and the experience of coming *out of* the world, and of being an indispensable element in its evolution.

Anyone who schools himself in the Way of archery trains himself in a sport which by no means repudiates the playful element inherent in all sports. At the same time, however, he schools himself in the path to self-knowledge, the Way to the primordial ground. That is one reason why Kyūdō is gradually becoming more popular in the West. Japanese archery, like other Budō sports, also accords with Western requirements. Kyūdō is more than just meditation in a restful sitting position, but it is not as movement-orientated as Kendō or Kung-fu either. In those movement-orientated Eastern sports, Western man runs the danger of getting so engrossed in learning their extreme rapidity of technique that he loses sight of the true objective. That goal involves maintaining a basically meditative attitude by calmly controlling one's movements, thereby discovering oneself. Judō provides the best example of an Eastern sport which has fallen away from this ideal. Everywhere in the world it has degenerated into little more than a struggle involving nothing but physical strength.

The Way of the Bow, on the other hand, will suit anyone who regards the purely meditative discipline of sitting still as too alien and 'passive', since Kyūdō harmoniously combines active and passive elements. It constitutes a way of 'movement in stillness' and in that respect resembles Chinese Tai'Chi or 'shadow-boxing' where all movements are made in slow motion for meditative reasons.

For the person handling the bow the only opponent to be faced and defeated is oneself. It is relatively easy to learn the basics of the purely technical requirements. So right from the start nothing prevents the archer from directing attention to both meditative essence and technique. Western behaviour patterns usually involve activity rather than the pure tranquillity of meditation in a seated position, but more and more people are rejecting the dynamic and outwardly directed character of Western sports, so the Way of the Bow may well offer the path of least difficulty since it is based on both action and meditative composure. If one always bears in mind during training that the path to self-knowledge can only become a reality if one is ready to work hard on oneself and with the bow, the danger of indulging in embarrassing pseudo-philosophising about the Way of the Bow will be kept within bounds from the start. That danger is basically greater in Kyūdō than in Kung-fu or Karate since archery lacks any adversary who will startle us out of our false dreams by launching a sudden physical attack.

If a Westerner takes up a Kyūdō bow, he should see it for what it is: a simple piece of bamboo and wood whose technical demands have to be mastered by the archer if he is serious about inner achievement. The archer should recognise that this instrument happens to come from the 'Far' East and has been in use there for centuries – among other things for this particular purpose – but that should not preoccupy him. In brief, any exotic feelings that might be evoked by this exceptionally long, elegantly curved piece of wood should be treated with cool detachment and allowed to fall away. It may be helpful for the archer to remember that he could basically pursue his aim equally well by using any other artefact familiar to him and his culture or by resorting to any other activity. If that were the case, it would, however, be necessary first to laboriously extract the meditative element, undoubtedly also originally inherent in some Western sports, from the tough husks of their orientation towards an outwardly measurable achievement. If he persists in that endeavour, he will, however, certainly soon come into conflict with the generally recognised objectives of the sport involved, whether it be football or fencing.

Since the archer has no immediate opponent apart from his little ego and ambition, it is basically easier for him to be on his guard against the ambition of *wanting* to hit the target as often as possible, which leads to one-sided concentration on technique. On the other hand, lack of an adversary is particularly problematic when the archer nevertheless succumbs to the ambition of wanting to score hits – to which he will be particularly prone in the early stages. As a result he will concentrate with all his might on the target – and still miss it. His shooting will turn into an embarrassingly forced activity which no blow or sudden attack by an opponent will help him overcome. In many cases he will not even become aware of the fact that his handling of the bow is rather questionable, unless his master or another experienced archer draws attention to the pointlessness of his involvement.

Any prospective Western Kyūdō archer who wishes to tread the

Way of the Bow without a master and in isolation from other bowmen, possibly with a target in the solitude of his own garden, will need a high degree of self-criticism and self-control. He should ask himself after each shot, coolly and without emotion, why he missed the target. In most cases he will realise that some form of false ambition made impossible the correct way of shooting from his centre. If the archer was successful in hitting the target, equal caution is required. A successful series of hits can all too easily lead to the illusion that one has attained some 'perfect' hits and is therefore definitely on the right way. It is, however, important to ascertain whether a hit originated in one's centre or was the chance outcome of conscious effort. If no master is available, the Western Kyūdō archer should at least practise as often as possible in the company of other archers whose criticism may keep him from the danger of wilfulness in his shooting practice. Their advice and corrections may also provide him with suggestions about the direction his self-criticism should take.

The danger of lapsing into exoticising attitudes is to a certain extent linked with one-sided and often romantically inclined pseudo-concentration on the philosophical aspects of archery, which have their roots in Taoism and Zen Buddhism. As we have more than once pointed out, body, technique, and mind/spirit, or action and thought, form an inseparable unity. Anyone who practises one aspect without paying equal attention to the others will therefore be taking a kind of breakneck leap into fatal self-deception. That has nothing in common with genuine Kyūdō. In real Kyūdō the technical aspects may appear to be subordinated to some extent to the spiritual element whose ultimate aim is self-knowledge and self-realisation, but that is not really the case. So-called 'spiritual' practice is nothing but mere pretense so long as the archer is incapable of successfully putting it to the test by way of satisfactory technical skill.

From the very beginning therefore, the Western bowman needs to dissociate himself from any deliberate focusing on results, so characteristic of his own culture, without, however, negating his own roots in that culture. At the same time he must not succumb – once he is holding the apparently so exotic bow in his hand – to the illusion that all technical effort is only of marginal importance since what really matters is to 'merge' with the 'spirit' of the bow. If he does not stumble over those dangerous obstacles, the archer will soon make considerable progress in terms of both sureness and striving on the way to his own centre – provided he persists in practising hard. Even though such progress should not affect him in any way, it will demonstrate that he is moving in the right direction, encouraging him to continue acting in a manner that has to be (and remain) free from self-will. Kyūdō is not meditation in the sense of liberation. Like any kind of meditation, it is only an aid on the way to that goal. Too much emphasis on the meditative aspect leads in most cases to a weakening of a hard struggle with oneself and the bow. Neglect of the meditative aspect, on the other hand, usually only produces sportsmen with impressive scores.

It might be thought that such problems do not exist for a Japanese archer, or at least only in exceptional cases. A brief glance at the more recent literature about Kyūdō will demonstrate the contrary, and a visit to any Kyūdō club will often only confirm that first impression. In Japan Kyūdō is well on the way towards becoming a Western-style sport. More recent books and today's training practices are primarily concerned with archery technique. Spiritual aspects are often only briefly touched on in the foreword or afterword. Even when they are mentioned in connection with practical training, the corresponding disciplines are practised less and less frequently. That change in Japanese Kyūdō, which is clearly seen and deplored by many, mostly older Japanese masters, is largely due to Japan's increasing orientation towards Western values. Externally measurable data and efficiency are beginning to count more than a deeper understanding – difficult to grasp externally – of the values of ancient Sino-Japanese traditions and Ways. That is also true of Japan's globally successful economy. Those traditions and Ways are now being rejected by large sections of Japan's youth as contrary to their frequently superficial individualistic values. While the West gradually seems to devote greater attention to the inner world and possible ways of reaching it, people in Japan are slowly leaving those Ways behind.

There are nevertheless still enough masters in Japan – whether in Kyūdō, the Way of Tea, or Kendō – who put as much stress on the spiritual element as on their teaching and practice of external and formal aspects. Any non-Japanese archer thus still has much to gain from spending at least six months in Japan in order to intensify his training under a Japanese master. D. T. Suzuki's suggestion that Japan should export its ancient arts to the West in order to receive them back later, purified of all externalities, seems to me somewhat premature in the case of Kyūdō – at least for the moment. In the context of Japanese reality the Western archer can rid himself of exoticising attitudes and of the illusion that his practice should be exclusively 'spiritual'. Even any average Japanese master will quickly teach him that the bow as such is nothing but an instrument. If it is not just to be played around with as some dreamlike and exotic toy, hard technical and mental work is necessary before the archer can penetrate to the spirit or heart of the bow, the *Yumi-no Kokoro*. If those conditions are fulfilled, Japanese archery will offer what we so desperately need in the Western world: an effective aid on the path towards harmonious unification of spirit and matter, and assistance on the Way towards the indivisible whole within ourselves.

PART IV

THE KYŪDŌ ARCHER'S EQUIPMENT

THE KYŪDŌ ARCHER'S EQUIPMENT

The Modern Kyūdō Bow

The Japanese bow (Jap. *yumi*; in its Sino-Japanese version *kyū*; in ancient times also called as *tarashi*) is the longest bow known to the world – longer even than the very effective English longbow of the fourteenth and fifteenth centuries which measured approximately 1.90 m. Three bows of differing lengths (according to the archer's height) are used today. The shortest measures 2.22 m., the longest 2.27 m. A fourth type (2.12 m. in length) is intended for children.

The fully drawn bow is half the archer's height, which is the basis for determining a suitable length. Today the average draw weight is usually between 16 and 20kg., depending on the archer's physical strength, but one frequently encounters archers who employ a bow with a draw weight of 25kg.

It is accepted today that the bow originally used in the Japanese archipelago – like the bow employed in Central and Northern Europe – was *not* a composite structure but made from a single piece of wood. That bow was in use from the Jōmon and Yayoi Era until the tenth and eleventh centuries. All reports to the contrary fail to take into account more recent Japanese archaeological discoveries. It was only in the eleventh century during the Heian Era (794–1192) when Japan intensified the import of cultural artefacts from China that methods enabling manufacture of composite bows were also adopted.

Today such bows are usually made from tough haze wood (a variety of waxwood or sumac: Talgsumach, *Rhus succedanen*,) and bamboo (Jap. *take*). They usually consist of a total of seven or eight laminations. Some bows, which are occasionally used by beginners today, are also made from fibre-glass. They are, of course, less expensive and less sensitive to wrong use. Their shooting characteristics also remain virtually unchanged even when the weather is unpropitious, while wooden bows suffer from high humidity. Any experienced archer will nevertheless possess at least two bows made from wood and bamboo, not necessarily because they are better but because the Japanese have a particular predilection for the simple elegance of natural materials. Much is also made of the original simplicity of all the equipment and utensils used in the other traditional arts from the Tea Ceremony to Shakuhachi music (played on a particular kind of bamboo flute). The artistic workmanship involved endows such artefacts with an unpretentious, natural elegance resulting from a process of refining what is natural in a spirit of simplicity and 'stillness'. The artefact thus remains genuine in its naturalness without, however, retaining its original rawness.

Despite its undeniably elegant form, the Japanese bow is ultimately nothing but a simple piece of wood and bamboo taken from nature. As such it is, however, alive, and tranquilly emanates something of the unadulterated purity of nature. Kyūdō is concerned with the purity of the primordial – both in the equipment employed and in man. The objective in both cases is the original form uncorrupted by anything that is not absolutely necessary. All the technical accessories which have virtually turned the Western bow into a perfect machine would be completely out of place in a Kyūdō bow. Such an emphasis would deprive the bow of its elegant natural simplicity, therefore hindering and distracting the archer on his way towards his own essential nature.

Just a word here about bamboo, whose symbolic significance is deeply rooted in Japanese thought. Bamboo is especially suitable for bows because of its extreme flexibility. The hardness of haze coupled with the pliability of bamboo constitute an almost ideal combination – not least in terms of the Yin and Yang principles. Bamboo is seen as symbolising easy adaptability and upright, honest sincerity. It bends patiently and modestly under even the heaviest load of snow when the inflexible branches of other trees have long started to break. At a particular, unforeseeable moment the bamboo lets the snow slip off, and energetically rebounds to its former position. It neither rebels against the weight of snow nor does it lose patience – and yet it remains firm and unbroken. Bamboo can also be very easily split lengthwise along a simple straight line. That combination of well-rounded, firm harmony and plain simplicity, based on inner strength, is precisely the quality that will best serve the archer in realisation of the steps leading up to the release and attainment of his own centre – or an outcome of such endeavours.

The most outstanding feature of the Kyūdō bow – apart from the length – is its mysterious asymmetrical shape, which has been the object of much speculation. Depictions on bronze bells from the Yayoi Era (c.250 BC – AD 300) and the testimony of a third-century Chinese historical work (*Gi-shin-toi-dan*) demonstrate that the Japanese bow has been asymmetrical since at least that time. Its upper limb down to the grip is about two and a half times as long as the lower limb. That characteristic feature is the outcome of Yayoi hunting methods – as previously described. It is often maintained that survival up to the present day of this bow results from its greater ease of handling on horseback. To a large extent that is certainly true. It can, however, be asked why shorter, symmetrical bows were not developed for such a purpose. One explanation is that what is already available and has proved its worth is seldom radically changed in Japan, but there seems to be another reason worth considering: the Japanese predilection for asymmetry as such, as manifested in Taoism and Zen.[1]

Asymmetry is a basic element in any thought and art influenced by Taoism and Zen. Zen Buddhism resulted from the fusion of Mahāyāna Buddhism and Taoism, but the former clearly preferred symmetry so the roots of asymmetry must be sought in Taoism. Confucianism, traditional Mahāyāna-Buddhism in China, and the art-works of the Nara Era in Japan (AD 710–794) are characterised by an aspiration to regularity and symmetry. Taoism, Zen, and the associated arts, on the other hand, avoid symmetry. That derives from the realisation that symmetry may well express something harmoniously rounded but such harmony is ultimately based on illusion and self-deception. The reconciliation of differences and the overcoming of antagonisms that symmetry strives to attain is too simple – perhaps even too facile – a solution. In both human relations and the interplay of all the elements at work in nature, symmetrical forms are the exception. Antagonisms and differences are therefore not artificially reconciled but allowed to exist. Asymmetry simply acknowledges the continued existence of opposites, but also recognises that such opposites are related to and need each other since one could not exist without the other.

Life and evolution would be inconceivable without asymmetry. Disparities are only different poles of one whole, poles that do not require resolution of apparent antagonism in 'beautiful' symmetry. Life, which springs from the interplay of different forces, would otherwise suffocate in symmetrical 'unification'. Symmetry is repetition. Repetition is the absolute antithesis of genuine life, true vitality, and any positive spontaneity. By offering pseudo-solutions symmetry ignores the insoluble mystery of existence which arouses a sense of creative wonder in us. It also fails to realise 'that the specific relationship, which should be of crucial importance to man, that is to say the relationship with what is explicity other, such as that between I and Thou, the human and the Divine, and immanence and transcendence, affecting freedom and demanding a clear-cut decision, can never be symmetrical'.[2]

To return to the bow itself – the wood from which it was made was as asymmetrical as a cloud or wave. That wood was alive and grew in accordance with the laws of nature, and not according to some artificial notion of those laws. That process of living, vital growth, and transformation whose understanding is so important to Taoism and Zen is illustrated in the Kyūdō bow's characteristic shape, which seems so odd to Westerners. If the bow is handled as a tool as it should be, the archer will be reminded at every training session that he must avoid the rigidities of skilful technical manipulation – and also that such practice is meant to lead to dynamic development. The archer must be in command of the technique. That is the prerequisite for the Way and demands constant practice – just as the bow itself came into being as the result of untiring work. It must, however, be remembered that the bow's asymmetrical shape did not come about because of Taoism and Zen since the Yayoi people knew of neither. Nevertheless, the fact that its dynamic form, which corresponds so closely to the nature of its use, has remained unchanged over a period of approximately 2,000 years is undoubtedly due to the influence of Taoism and Zen.

The basically rather impractical length of the bow can also be seen as a challenge to use it correctly. Its extreme dimensions force the archer to treat the bow with utmost circumspection and care at all times. Even taking the bow out of its stand, carrying, and handling it demands vigilance and mindfulness since it can easily knock against things and obstruct other archers, thereby disturbing the peaceful atmosphere in the training hall (dōjō).

From the very beginning such wide-awake mindfulness leads the archer to sharpen his senses for those externalities so that he may no longer be distracted by them.

In former times a strip of brocade was wound around the grip on top of a thin piece of paper containing an invocation or glorification of the God Aizen-myoo. That brocade was red since red was Aizen-myoo's colour. A strip of leather finally covered everything else. Purple leather was exclusively reserved for the Shōgun, and feudal lords usually chose black. Today the archer is not bound by any regulations, and purple, blue, brown, black, and dark green are widely used. If he so wishes, any customer who commissions a bow from a bow-maker can have an invocation to the god inserted under the leather of the grip. That is usually first taken to a temple for consecration.

Although that basic shape is characteristic of Kyūdō bows, a number of slight variations are in use, developed by different schools and local traditions. Those variants usually involve the curves of the bow. All such forms are harmonious within themselves – provided the bow is a good one – but they differ, albeit only slightly, in terms of the character of the shot attained. The fact that those forms do indeed date back to ancient traditions is demonstrated by their mention as early as the *Yo-sha-roku*, a work about the bow which appeared in 1675.[3] Morikawa Kosan, the bow-master who coined the expression Kyūdō and founded the old Yamato school, is reputed to have entrusted a document bearing that title to Hirose Yoichi, who then proceeded to publish it under his own name.

Whatever the shape of a bow, it is generally thought to meet the requirements if its four main curves are balanced in a harmonious and dynamic way. Those curves are:

1. Hime-zori (Princess curve);
2. Tori-uchi (Literally 'Bird-Eater');
3. Koshi-zori (Hip curve);
   or Shimo-no-nari (Lower curve);
4. Ko-zori (Little curve).

The price of a bow is essentially determined by the degree to which its curves are dynamically balanced.

Every archer should possess at least two and preferably three bows, especially if he practises every day as he really ought to. There is a reason for that. If a bow is in constant use, the character

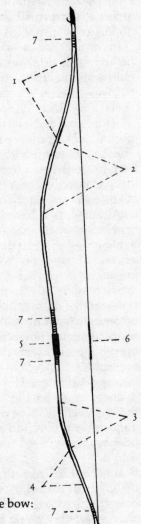

The Kyūdō Bow

The four curves influencing the quality of the bow:
1. *Hime-zori* (Princess curve)
2. *Tori-uchi* ('Bird-Eater')
3. *Shimo-no-nari* (Lower curve) – or
   Koshi-zori (Hip curve)
4. *Ko-zori* (Little curve)
5. *Nigiri* (Grip)
6. *Naka-shikake* (Strengthening for the bowstring where the arrow is nocked)
7. Binding

of the shots attainable with it will alter after about a year, and the bow will need a rest of about twelve but preferably eighteen months.

The archer will also use his second bow for about a year, and then return to the first one. Today a good bow costs about 50,000 Yen (approximately 350 US dollars).

The Bowstring

Bowstrings *(tsuru)* are made as in former times from long hemp threads and mostly still twisted by hand. They are rubbed with a mixture of resin and cedar oil so as to increase durability, particularly with regard to damp. Machine-made bowstrings are now available too, but archers still prefer those made by hand. Synthetic strings are occasionally used, but I myself have only seen such strings on two or three occasions during my years of practice. There also exist woven strings which are stronger than the twisted ones, but were already unpopular in ancient times because they were made by women. Weapons were supposed not to come into contact with women. If they did, they were thereafter regarded as unclean and useless. Today the Way of the Bow is open to men and women alike so there is no longer any basis for such an aversion. Bowstrings – albeit only the twisted variety – are thus now produced by both female and male artisans.

There is another reason why Japanese Kyūdō archers have for many centuries preferred twisted hemp-strings which tear easily. Taosim and Zen attach no importance to durability and permanence. On the contrary they affirm frailty, change, and death as embodiments of the natural rhythms of the universe. Beauty and propriety are ascribed to whatever manifests this ubiquitous rhythm most strikingly. It happens to be in the bowstring's nature to let the arrow fly from the bow and to break after a certain time. If in daily use, it will at most last for two months. A Taoist or Zen Buddhist would think it rather 'childish' to try and by-pass that natural factor by using artificial materials. Instead of accepting the ephemerality of natural hemp, one would thus yield, out of purely practical and materialistic considerations, to the cheap advantages of artificial materials, succumbing to illusion. Breaking is inherent in a string's nature.

I have seen archers scrutinise their bowstring, wondering how it

155

could still be usable after unusually prolonged service. If a bowstring suddenly snaps when the bow is fully drawn, producing a strangely harsh cutting sound, many archers take that as an admonition never to falter in their efforts and under no circumstances to fall victim to the illusion that nothing but a succession of good shots is required for attainment of their goal. When an archer rests on his laurels, the snapping of the bowstring and its cutting sound are supposed to blast him out of his complacency and to shatter his false, egocentric ambition about hitting the target. The sharp unpleasant sound is said to snatch the archer from the abyss of any incorrect mental attitude – particularly from that of illusion, self-deception, and misguided romanticising – and to bring him back to the harsh reality of practical training, in the same way as a flash of lightning suddenly floods the night with bright light.

The string is strengthened – from approximately 1 to 2 cm. above the nocking point *(naka-shikake)* where the arrow is set on the string to about 7 or 8 cm. below that – with hemp-threads especially produced for that purpose, or with reconditioned fibres from already torn strings. That allows the arrow to be firmly lodged in position, prevents the hard slot in the arrow tail from damaging the string, and ensures that the string can be securely fitted into the notch of the shooting glove *(yugake)* without coming to harm. Before the hemp-threads are wrapped around the string, the latter is coated with special glue. While the section thus strengthened is still wet, it is rubbed between two flat pieces of wood *(doho)* until it is smooth and rounded. Kyūdō archers prefer relatively thin strings because they produce an exceedingly pleasant sound when an arrow is discharged – provided it was released in accordance with correct technique and the right spiritual attitude. Experienced masters only have to listen to that sound in order to determine whether the release was altogether satisfactory or a failure. They need not have seen either the archer or the target.

The Arrows

If the great variety of arrows used in former times is compared with the arrows *(ya)* employed today, hardly any changes will be ascertained over the centuries.

When the Japanese began to import the laminated (composite) bow and its method of manufacture from China, they also adopted the Chinese way of making arrows. It seems that the initial preference was for the light and pliable wood of the willow, but bamboo was already utilised too. Nowadays good quality arrows are almost all made from a special variety of bamboo – or rather only from its two-year-old shoots – whose flexibility and suppleness provide ease of working and prime durability.

After having been cut, such bamboo is left to dry for about six to eight months. As a result it shrinks a little in length and diameter. At the end of that period the first work process, called *neru* (kneading) takes place. The arrow, which is still slightly bent, is straightened above a charcoal fire. Bamboo can easily be shaped and hardened above a fire, which explains – in conjunction with its symbolic value – why it is employed for bows and arrows as well as being omnipresent in Japanese everyday existence.

The *neru* stage is followed by the *ara-dame* (rough improvement). The surface of the arrow, by then more or less straight, is carefully worked on with a scraping blade. That step is followed by the *naka-dame* (further improvement) when the arrow is once again treated above a charcoal fire until it is absolutely straight. Its surface is smoothed down at the same time until no rough passages are visible any more. After cooling down, the shaft has attained an ultimate degree of hardness.

During the final *ishi-arai* stage (*ishi*, stone; *arai*, washing) the arrow is polished for the last time. That is done by pulling the arrow-shaft through the grooves of an oval stone while fine sand, serving as an abrasive, smooths and polishes its entire surface. Finally the shaft is oiled or varnished in order to weatherproof it still further.

The arrow made in that way is called *ya-no chiku*. The shafts vary in diameter. Those of the same diameter throughout their length are called *ichi-monji*. That term derives from the Japanese character for the number one, *ichi*, which is represented by a simple horizontal line. The *ichi-monji* is the standard type of arrow today. There are also arrows *(mugi-tsubo*, grain of wheat) tapering from mid-length towards the tip and tail. That type is particularly suitable for *enteki* shooting (over a distance of 60 m.) since its centre of gravity is in the middle during flight. The third variety of arrow found today, *sugi-nari* (a term indicating its conical, cedar-like shape), is widest at the front and narrowest at the tail end of the shaft, which is well suited to normal target shooting, i.e. for shorter distances.

The 2–5 mm. deep nocks *(hazu)* once used to consist of a bamboo ring provided with a notch attached to the end of the shaft. There were also nocks which were cut directly into the tail end of the arrow-shaft. Today pieces of horn with a slot cut into them are inserted into the shaft, and are used almost exclusively.

Different bindings used to be employed for securing the feathers and arrowheads, and also for strengthening the tail-end of the shaft. Their numerous names depended on the material used (e.g. silk thread, paper, bark, varnished binding) and their particular purpose. Nowadays there are two sorts of bindings for securing the feathers and one for strengthening the tail-end of the shaft where the nock is inserted. The *moto-hagi* secures the front end of the quill, and the *ura-hagi* the quill above the back end. The binding which strengthens the nock end of the shaft is called *hazu-maki*.

The feathers *(hane)* of many different kinds of birds have been used since ancient times for stabilising the arrow's flight, but the preference was for birds of prey. The outer tail feathers of the eagle were particularly sought after because of their hardness and durability. Those are characteristically called *ishi-uchi*, 'Falling Stones'. The feathers of hawks, harriers, cranes, wild geese, ravens, and even chickens fulfil the same purpose though. Owl feathers must not, however, be used for arrows since the owl is believed to be associated with all kinds of bad omens.

The outer tail feathers are best, followed by those from the middle and inside of the wing. The others are too soft. From an aesthetic point of view, feathers are distinguished according to their colour and patterning, which should match as closely as possible in a set of four arrows.

Today such a set of average good quality bamboo arrows costs the equivalent of between 50 and 80 US dollars in Japan. Four high-quality bamboo arrows with eagle feathers of the same colour and marking can, however, easily fetch well over 1000 dollars. That explains why cheaper aluminium arrows with less precious feathers, costing around 50 dollars, are used more and more frequently in regular target practice. Experienced Kyūdōka also possess at least one set of good bamboo arrows for competitions and other special occasions.

Two of the arrows in a set are called *haya*, and the other two *otoya.* The curvature of the feathers attached to the *haya* always points towards the archer when the arrow has been placed on the string. With the *otoya* the slight curve points outwards. A *haya* is used first and then an *otoya* as a matter of principle. There is a reason why the feathers are positioned so that their curvatures point in different directions. Two arrows released by the archer in exactly the same way should never hit the same spot. Every arrow's point of impact will be minimally different – thanks to the different curvature of the feathers. The second arrow will therefore never hit the first, and thus cannot damage its precious feathers. Nowadays arrowheads are called *ne* (root) or *ita tsuki*. In former times they were known as *yajiri*, demonstrating a variety of forms ranging from forked or pointed heads and barbed 'gut lacerators' *(watakuri)* to massive fully rounded ones. Today simple iron points are generally employed. The diameter is the same as that of the front end of the shaft while the tip itself is sharply pointed. The arrows used for practising at the *makiwara*, the straw bundle, are rounded off smoothly. That kind of arrow also has no feathers. The Kyūdō arrow is considerably longer than that used in Western archery since the bowstring is pulled back to behind the right ear when drawn. Its length is determined by taking half the archer's height and adding approximately 8 to 10 cm. to that measurement.

Today arrows are kept in what is known as the *yatsuzu* (arrow cylinder), a slim tube made of hard cardboard which widens towards the top because the feathers take up more space than the arrow-heads. This cardboard tube is given a simple coat of varnish, and is usually also strengthened and decorated with *tō* binding *(Calamus rotang*, feather palm), thin strips of bamboo, cherrywood bark, or something similar. In the old days Samurai mostly used the open *ebira*, a small wooden box covered with the hide of boar or bear, animals which were regarded as courageous because they never retreated. Such a box was about 15 cm. high with a rack mounting fitted inside and could carry up to forty arrows. Cords and a hoop fixed to its back kept the arrows in position. The Samurai fastened such an open quiver to his right hip.

There was also the *shiko,* an open arrow-case made from simple bamboo, which was not a quiver in the usual sense. That *shiko* was suspended on the left hip from a hook on the belt.

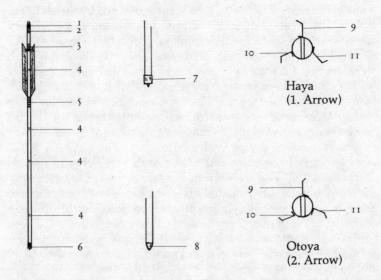

Haya
(1. Arrow)

Otoya
(2. Arrow)

The Kyūdō Arrow

1. *Hazu* (Nock)
2. *Hazumaki* (Binding for the nock)
3. *Urahagi* (Upper feather binding)
4. The four joints (knots) in the bamboo arrow from above: *Hanaka-bushi, Sodezuri-bushi, Nonaka-bushi, Itsuke-bushi*
5. *Moto-hagi* (Lower feather binding)
6. *Itatsuki* (Arrowhead)
7. Tip of the arrow used today for shooting at targets
8. Tip of the arrow used for *makiwara* practice, rounded so as to preserve the straw bundle
9. *Hashiri-ba* (Main feather)
10. *Yuzuri-ba* (Inner feather)
11. *Togake-ba* (Outer feather)

●

The Archery Glove

The glove *(yugake)* covers the thumb, index, and middle finger of the right hand. It is available in goat, pigskin, and considerably more durable deer or antelope hide. A piece of wood or horn is inserted beneath the thumb, protecting it against being injured by the bowstring, and also keeping it rigid. The thumb in warriors' gloves of old was soft since the archer also had to use the right hand for his sword. Gloves for shooting on horseback still have a soft thumb today so that the rider can guide his horse when not using the bow. While shooting he will of course rely solely on his thighs.

The most important part of the glove is the notch into which the bow-string is inserted when the bow is drawn. For normal target practice in the *Heki* school that slot is at right angles to the thumb axis. Other schools may prefer different types of notches, Bowstring notches which are positioned at an angle of about 110 or even 135 degrees in relation to the thumb axis are suitable for long-distance shooting *(enteki,* 60 m.). A simple thin cotton glove, which can easily be washed, is worn underneath the leather glove in order to protect the precious leather against perspiration and dirt.

When putting on his glove the archer will, as a matter of principle, kneel with his face turned towards the target. He must never be standing at that point.

●

Clothing

Although Kyūdō can be practised in any sports clothes, traditional clothing is obligatory in Japan for regular training sessions and particularly for competitions and ceremonies. That consists of a white shirt *(gi* – the man's shirt has holes underneath the armpit for better ventilation but the woman's garment does not), a kind of culotte *(hakama)*, a wide belt *(obi)*, and single-toed (for the big toe) white socks *(tabi)*. In addition women wear a breast protector *(mune-ate)* made of leather. The *hakama* for women have no *hakama-no shita* (a trapezoid back-piece). Their

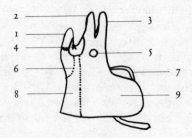

seen from outside

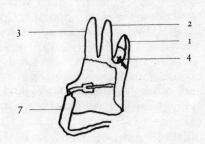

seen from inside

The Archery Glove

1. The thumb beneath whose tough outer leather a piece of horn or wood is also inserted
2. Index finger
3. Middle finger
4. *Tsuru-makura* (Nock into which the bowstring is inserted)
5. *Mon* (Family coat of arms)
6. Seams
7. *Himo* (Cord for fastening the glove)
8. Hard, unsupple leather
9. Soft, pliable leather

waist-band is instead wider at the back. The ladies' *obi* is shorter than the men's.

In ceremonial archery *(sharei)* a kimono is worn above a lighter under-kimono *(monpu-ku)* instead of the *gi*. The wide sleeves of the kimono naturally tend to get in the way. That is why men take their left arm out of the kimono, while women solve the problem by tying the wide sleeves back with a special cord which is usually white.

Those traditional garments are worn both in winter and in summer. The thin white *gi* appears to be too cold in winter, but the experienced archer creates the necessary warmth for himself by way of concentrated abdominal breathing. For the beginner that time of year is the best opportunity for learning and practising how to apply such breathing in order to produce the necessary amount of heat energy. One may wonder about Kyūdōkas' great fondness for traditional clothing, which to some extent resembles that of former Samurai – especially in view of the fact that traditional clothing is hardly ever come across in everyday Japanese life. It is only worn on festive occasions, and even then more and more Japanese men prefer to wear Western suits.

Well-founded practical considerations rather than traditionalism lie behind retention of the customary attire for Kyūdō and other traditional Ways and Budō sports. Out Western clothing is relatively close-fitting and free bodily movements are therefore to some extent impeded, especially at the extremities. In addition – and this is far more serious – Western clothing does not allow the physical and spiritual energy to flow freely through the body. If trousers, shirts, and belts are too tight, the subtle energy which archers develop through their practice is checked and dammed up. It is then very difficult to direct that energy to those parts of the body where it is needed. Traditional Japanese clothes are without exception loose-fitting and thus especially well-suited for meditation and Budō sports.

●

The Training Hall

Kyūdō is practised in a hall *(dōjō, kyūdōjō)* which in former times was made entirely of wood. The interior fittings, especially the floor, still consist of wood, even though concrete and stone buildings are also to be found today. The polished wooden floor is raised about 10 to 15 cm. above the ground beneath. One of the hall's long sides consists of wooden sliding doors which are opened before target practice begins, revealing the shooting area. The archers thus shoot from the inside at a target outside, that is to say at a disc 36 cm. in diameter which is set up under a roof at a distance of exactly 28.44 m. The area between the hall and the targets is open to the sky and usually consists of a closely mown lawn. As a rule there is a single low evergreen bush at the left side of the area between hall and targets, which transforms the symmetry of that space into asymmetry. Kyūdō can therefore be practised at any time of year and in all weathers.

Archery which takes place completely out in the open always involves longer distances (usually 60 m. in what is known as *enteki* shooting). In that case the target disc is 1.58 m. in diameter.

On entering their *dōjō* archers first bow to the *kamiza*, a platform erected in front of the right end of the hall and raised about 30 cm. above the floor. That is where the master and guests of honour – and during competitions the judges – squat on straw mats. That end-wall is also usually embellished with calligraphy relating to the philosophy of Kyūdō (in the author's training hall, for instance, the maxim 'Movement in Stillness'), the photograph of an old master associated with the hall, and often a small shrine. A magnificent symbolic arch is often erected there too. Its impact is sometimes attractively enhanced with an ikebana flower arrangement. At the opposite end of the hall the *makiwara* are placed at eye level. Before starting his actual target practice the archer will discharge a few preliminary shots at them from a distance of about 2 metres. That preliminary practice is of great importance because it serves as mental preparation leading to the harmonisation of mind, body, and bow. The master will also check the archer's technique and mental attitude during that warming-up period. In addition it is a matter of principle that the training session be brought to a close by a few shots at the *makiwara* following the target practice itself.

The structure, fittings, and layout of the hall are asymmetrical, endowing it with a particular vitality exerting a positive and stimulating effect on the archer.

The fact that the hall is obviously always open during target practice ensures its own and the archers' integration into nature. The hall appears to be nothing but a makeshift expedient, simply needed for shooting but with no claim to any outstanding value in itself. That integration in nature is further accentuated by the hall's wooden furnishings and the fact that all the equipment, from the bow and its stand to the *makiwara*, is made of natural materials.

DEBTS OF GRATITUDE

The coming into being of this book owes particularly much to my two masters, Isamu Masuda and Masato Muramoto, who have for years guided me along the Way of the Bow and will hopefully long continue to do so. They helped me see the value of this Way with the inner eye.

Professor Yoshio Takahashi helped me discover hidden treasures in Japan's unique Tenri Library, and some of those ancient works contributed essentially to this book. He also made available his room in the library when my own could not be used for a considerable time.

Thanks are also due to Professor Shigeo Yamaguchi for his untiring readiness to clarify individual questions about Zen Buddhism in a reciprocal exchange of views.

Professor Hiroshi Kanaseki, an archaeologist whose fame extends beyond Japan, contributed much to the section on the history of the bow, particularly with regard to the Jōmon and Yayoi epochs.

I must thank Gerd Lorenz, my friend and companion on the Ways of Tao, Zen, and Tantra, which for us essentially constitute a whole, for a number of fruitful ideas about the interrelationship between breathing, energy, and meditation.

My colleague, Professor Hirotake Takita, made it possible for me to devote myself to this book alongside my teaching duties without coming under pressure.

Thanks, too, to Professor Dr Robert Schinzinger for his preface to the book.

I should also like to express my gratitude to Masuko, who patiently assisted me when difficulties arose in the translation of older Japanese texts.

And my apologies go to Yukiko Nina and Andreas Masayumi for the fact that their interests were often neglected when I was working on this book.

Illustrations 2, 4, 10, 11, 12, 13, 16 and 18 are reproduced by kind permission of the All-Japanese Kyūdō Association from *Kyūdō-Hassetsu*, Zen Nippon Kyūdō Remmei, Tōkyō, 1981.

SELECTED GLOSSARY

aosō (or kanakosō)   – A kind of hemp used for the bowstring.

ara-dame   – 'Rough improvement'. The second stage in producing a bamboo arrow. Scraping the shaft with a fine blade.

ariake   – 'Moon at daybreak'; method of aiming so that the full target is seen to the left of the bow.

ashibumi   – The stance. The first stage of 'hassetsu'.

budō   – The traditional martial arts.

chichi-haha-no osamari   – See 'sō-no osamari'.

daisan-no tsuriai   – Unity and balance between the bow-hand and the right hand just before release of the arrow.

dō   – From the Chinese 'Tao', signifying 'Way' or 'Path'. In Kyūdō it denotes all that is involved in handling the bow as a way and means of rounding off and maturing the archer's personality. Thus also a Way towards self-knowledge and self-realisation.

dōjō   – The practice hall.

dōzukuri   – The balance of the trunk. Placing the body squarely on the support afforded by the legs. The second stage of 'hassetsu'.

ebira   – An open arrow quiver used in old times by the samurai.

enteki   – Long-distance shooting (60 m.).

fuse-dake-yumi   – Composite bows. In Japan first produced during the Heian period (794–1192).

gi   – Shirt.

gobu-no tsume   – The five-part finish ending the 'kai' stage.

167

hagi	– Arrow bindings.
hakama	– A kind of culotte.
hakama-no shita	– A trapezoid back-piece.
hanare	– The release. The seventh stage of 'hassetsu'.
hane	– Feather.
hassetsu	– The eight stages leading to release of the arrow and stepping back from the shooting-position.
haya	– Arrows whose feathers point towards the archer when placed on the string. Always the first arrows used in shooting.
haze	– A variety of waxwood used in making the bow.
hazu	– The nock of the arrow.
hazu-maki	– Arrow binding that secures the nock end of the shaft.
hikiwake	– The draw.
hineri	– The right forearm and the right hand are slightly rotated inwards towards the trunk during the final moments of 'kai'.
honza	– Preparatory line in the practice hall.
hozuke	– When the bow is fully drawn the shaft of the arrow lightly touches the corner of the archer's mouth.
ichi-monji	– Arrows with the same diameter throughout their length.
ishi-arai	– 'Stone-washing'; the last step in producing a bamboo arrow. Polishing of the shaft by pulling it through the grooves of an oval stone.
ishi-uchi	– The outer tail feathers of the eagle. Particularly sought after because of their hardness and durability. Most expensive.
ita-tsuki	– The arrowhead.
jiman	– See 'kai'.

168

SELECTED GLOSSARY

kai
— The final concentration and chest effort in completing the full draw. The sixth stage of 'hassetsu'.

kamiza
— Platform in the dōjō where the masters and guests of honour are seated.

ki
— Breath or a kind of spiritual nervous energy located below the naval in the 'tanden' (Chin. *ch'i*).

ki-kai
— 'The Ocean of Breath', see 'tanden' (Chin. *ch'i-hai*).

kyū
— The bow (Sino-jap. reading).

Kyūdō
— The 'Way of the Bow'.

kyūdō-ka
— The 'Man of the Bow'. Someone who pursues the Way of the Bow.

kyū-jutsu
— The art of archery, putting greater stress on artistic and technical aspects rather than on the concept of the 'Way'.

makiwara
— Practice target consisting of a tightly bound bundle of straw.

mato
— The target.

mikomi
— Final stage of viewing the mark.

minarai
— Learning by seeing and copying the master's actions.

mizunagare
— The position of the arrow during the *uchiokoshi* and *hikiwake*.

monomi
— Viewing the mark.

monpuku
— Light under-kimono used in ceremonial kyūdō instead of the 'gi'.

motohagi
— Arrow binding that secures the front end of the quill.

mugi-tsubo
— Arrows tapering from mid-length towards the tip and tail.

mune-ate
— Breast protector (for women).

mushin
— Mental detachment. Unconditional freedom of spirit which Zen Buddhism views as a precondition for advancement towards

enlightenment. Applied to kyūdō, mushin entails implementation of the entire process leading up to the release with an undivided consciousness, undistracted by discursive thought.

naka-dame	– 'Further improvement'. Third step in producing a bamboo arrow. The arrow is treated above a charcoal fire until it is absolutely straight. Then its surface is smoothed.
naka-shikake	– Strengthening of the bowstring where the arrow is nocked.
ne	– The arrowhead.
neru	– 'Kneading', the first step in producing a bamboo arrow. The arrow gets its approximate form by being bent above a charcoal fire.
nigiri	– The grip of the bow.
nobiai (nobi)	– See 'kai'.
obi	– Belt.
otoya	– Arrows whose feathers point slightly outwards when placed on the string. Always used after the 'haya'.
ryū	– A school of training as in Heki-ryū and Ogasawara-ryū.
sha-i	– Shooting line in the practice hall.
sharei	– A ceremonial form of Kyūdō which originated in the Japanese court around the fifth century.
shiko	– A kind of open quiver used by samurai.
sō-no osamari	– Final position and balance between the bow-hand and the right hand just before release of the arrow.
sugi-nari	– Arrows of conical shape, widest at the front and narrowest at the tail.
tabi	– Socks.
tachi-rei	– Bowing in the direction of the target while standing.

SELECTED GLOSSARY

take	– Bamboo. For the characteristics of this material see the chapter 'The Modern Kyūdō Bow'.
tanden	– A point about 3–5 cm. below the navel. Centre of the body and the spirit. All bodily movements derive from the tanden, and all spiritual activities should be concentrated on this point. The tanden is above all the centre for embryonic abdominal breathing.
tarashi	– Ancient term for bow.
tenouchi	– Gripping the bow.
tō	– Feather palm, calamus rotang, used for the binding on arrow cylinders.
torikake	– Grasping the bowstring.
tsuruai	– Balance between the bow-arm and the right arm.
tsuru	– The bowstring.
tsuru-makura	– Nock of the glove into which the bowstring is inserted.
uchiokoshi	– The raising of the bow. The fourth stage of 'hassetsu'.
ura-hagi	– Arrow binding that secures the quill above the back end.
ya	– Arrow.
yabusame	– Archery from horseback.
yagoro	– The utmost degree of concentration of mind and power during the 'kai' stage.
yajiri	– Arrowhead (like 'ne' and 'ita-tsuki').
yami	– The 'eclipse' method of aiming. The target is hidden behind the bow.
ya-no chiku	– The traditional process of producing a bamboo arrow.
yatsuzu	– Arrow cylinder.
yazuka	– Arrow length.

yudaoshi	– Lowering of the bow after release of the arrow.
yugaeri	– The 'return' of the bow. At the moment when the arrow has been released, the power of the rebounding bowstring causes the bow to rotate to the left so that the string hits the outside of the bow-arm. No shot is complete without this 'yugaeri'.
yugake	– The glove used in Kyūdō.
yugamae	– Setting the bow in place. Being prepared. The third stage of 'hassetsu'.
yumi	– The bow.
yumi no kokoro	– The spirit inherent in the bow, 'the heart of the bow'.
yunde	– The bow-hand; the hand holding the bow (normally the left hand).
Zanshin	– The state of body and mind after release of the arrow.
Za-zen	– 'Sitting Zen', the meditation used in Zen Buddhism.
Zen Buddhism	– A school of Buddhism brought into Japan in the twelfth century.

SELECTED BIBLIOGRAPHY

Acker, R. B., *Japanese Archery*, Tuttle, Rutland and Tokyo, 1965.

Anesaki, Masaharu, *History of Japanese Religion*, Tuttle, Rutland and Tokyo, 1963.

Aston, W. G., *Nihongi – Chronicles of Japan from the Earliest Times to AD 697*, Tuttle, Tokyo 1972.

Bellah, Robert N., *Tokugawa Religion – The Values of Preindustrial Japan*, Chicago, 1961.

Bersihand, Roger, *Histoire du Japon des origines à nos jours*, Payot, Paris, 1959.

Blofeld, John, *The Way of Power*, Allen & Unwin, London, 1970.

_____ *The Secret and Sublime*, Allen & Unwin, London, 1973.

Blyth, R. H., *Zen and Zen Classics* Vols. 1–5, Hokuseido Press, Tokyo 1960–70.

Chander, Yogacharya Ramesh, *Tantric Yoga, Techniques and Rituals for Health, Wealth, Success*, New Delhi.

Chang Chung-yuang, *Creativity and Taoism*, Julian Press, New York, 1963.

Chia, Mantak, *Awaken Healing Energy through the Tao – the Taoist Secret of Circulating Internal Power*, Aurora Press, New York, 1983.

Chuang Tzu, *Chuang Tzu, Taoist Philosopher and Chinese Mystic*, Allen & Unwin, London, 1961.

Colegrave, Sukie, *The Spirit of the Valley*, Virago, London, 1979.

Confucius, *The Analects*, Penguin Books, Harmondsworth.

Cooper, J. C., *Taoism, The Way of the Mystic*, 1972.

Deshimaru-Roshi, Taisen, *The Zen Way to the Martial Arts*, Rider, London, 1983.

_____ *Questions to a Zen Master*, Rider, London, 1985.

_____ *La Pratique du Zen*, Edition Seghers, Paris, 1977.

Dumoulin/Fuller-Sasaki, *The Development of Chinese Zen after the Sixth Patriarch in the Light of Mumokuan*, New York, 1953.

Dürckheim, Karlfried Graf von, *Hara: The Vital Centre of Man*, Unwin Books, London, 1985.

Eliade, Mircea, *Yoga, Immortality and Freedom*, Bollingen Series LVI, Princeton University Press, Princeton, 1969.

Giles, Herbert A. (transl.), *Chuang Tzu – Mystic, Moralist and Social Reformer*, Shanghai, 1926.

Giles, Lionel (transl.) *The Sayings of Lao-Tzu*, London, 1905.

_____ *Taoist Teachings from the Book of Lieh Tzu*, reprinted by Allen & Unwin, London, 1947.

Groot, Gerard J., *The Prehistory of Japan*, New York, 1951.

de Groot, J. J. M., *The Religious System of China*, Leiden 1892 – 1910.

_____ *Religion in China. Universism: A Key to the Study of Taoism and Confucianism*, C. P. Putnam's Sons, New York and London, 1912.

van Gulik, R. H., *Sexual Life in Ancient China*, E. J. Brill, Leiden, 1961 (reprinted 1974).

Hall, John Whitney, *Japanese History, Guide to Japanese Reference and Research Materials*, London, 1954.

Hall/Beardsley, *Twelve Doors to Japan*, New York and London, 1965.

Heath, E. G., *Grey Goose Wing – A History of Archery*, New York Graphic Society, 1968.

Herrigel, Eugen, *Zen in the Art of Archery*, transl. R. F. C. Hull, Vintage/Random, New York, 1971.

Hirai, Tomio, *Zen Meditation Therapy*, Japan Publications, Tokyo, 1975.

Holmes/Horioka, *Zen Art for Meditation*, Tuttle, Rutland and Tokyo, 1973.

Hoover, Thomas, *Zen Culture*, Random House, New York, 1977.

Lao-Tzu, *Tao Te Ching*, transl. Gia-Fu Feng and Jane English, Wildwood House, London, 1972.

Legge, James (transl.), *Confucian Analects, The Great Learning, The Doctrine of the Mean*, Oxford, 1893.

⸺ *Taoi Te Ching and the Writings of Chuang Tzu*, new edition, Taipei, 1963.

Lieh-tzu, *The Book of Lieh-tzu*, transl. A. C. Graham, London, 1960.

Lin Yutang, *The Wisdom of Laotse*, Random House, New York, 1948.

Lysebeth, André van, *Pranayama: Yoga of Breathing*, Allen & Unwin, London.

McCullough, Helen and Craig (transl.), *The Taiheiki, A Chronicle of Mediaeval Japan*, Columbia University Press, New York, 1959 (Tuttle 1979/81).

Musashi, Miyamoto, *A Book of Five Rings*, Allison & Busby, London, 1974.

Needham, Joseph, *Science and Civilisation in China*, Cambridge University Press, 1956.

Nippon Budokan, The, *Budo Demonstration, the Games of the 18th Olympiad*, Tokyo, 1964.

Nitobe, Inazo, *Bushido – The Soul of Japan*, Tuttle, Rutland and Tokyo, 1969.

Northrop, F. S. C., *The Meeting of East and West*, Macmillan, New York, 1946.

Okakura, Kakuzō, *The Book of Tea*, Tuttle, Rutland, 1956.

Ono, Dr Sokyo, *Shinto – The Kami Way*, Tuttle, Rutland and Tokyo, 1962.

Pálos, Stephan, *The Chinese Art of Healing*, New York, 1971/72.

Philippi, Donald L. (transl.), *Kojiki*, University of Tokyo Press, 1968.

Pirsig, Robert M., *Zen and the Art of Motorcycle Maintenance*, 1974.

Pi yen lu, *The Blue Cliff Record*, transl. by T. and J. C. Cleary, Shambala, Boulder and London, 1977.

Radhakrishnan, Sarvepalli (ed.), *History of Philosophy Eastern and Western*, 2 vols., London and New York, 1952.

Ramacharaka, Yogi, *Hatha Yoga Or the Yogi Philosophy of Physical Well-Being*, Fowler, London.

Ratti/Westbrook, *Secrets of the Samurai*, Tuttle, Tokyo, 1973.

Reischauer, E. O., *Japan – Past and Present*, Knopf, New York, 1967.

Robinson, Russel, *Japanese Arms and Armour*, London, 1969.

Sadler, A. L., *Cha-no-yu*, Tuttle, Tokyo, 1962.

Sansom, George B., *The Western World and Japan*, Knopf, New York, 1950.

⸺ *A History of Japan to 1334*, Stanford, Calif., 1958.

⸺ *A History of Japan 1334–1615*, Stanford, 1960.

⸺ *Japan, A Short Cultural History*, rev. edn, Cresset Press, London, 1962.

⸺ *A History of Japan 1615–1817*, Stanford, 1963.

Sekida, Katsuki, *Zen Training – Methods and Philosophy*, Weatherhill, New York and Tokyo, 1975.

SELECTED BIBLIOGRAPHY

Sekiguchi, Shindai, *Zen, A Manual for Westerners*, Japan Publications, Tokyo, 1970.

Shibayama, Zenkei, Abbot, *A Flower Does Not Speak: Zen Essays*, Tuttle, Rutland and Tokyo, 1970.

Sollier/Gyorbiro, *Japanese Archery – Zen in Action*, Weatherhill, Tokyo and New York, 1969.

Suzuki, Daisetz T., *Training of the Zen Buddhist Monk*, Eastern Buddhist Society, Kyoto, 1934.

_____ *The Zen Doctrine of No-Mind*, Rider, London, 1949.

_____ *Mysticism: Christian and Buddhist*, George Allen & Unwin, London, 1957.

_____ *An Introduction to Zen Buddhism*, Arrow Books, London, 1959.

Suzuki, Shunryu, *Zen Mind – Beginner's Mind*, Weatherhill, Tokyo and New York, 1970.

Tiwald, Horst, *Psycho-training im Kampf- und Budo-Sport*, Ahrensburg, 1981.

Trevor, M. H. (transl.) *The Ox and His Herdsman*, Hokuseido Press, Tokyo, 1969.

Tsunetomo, Yamamoto, *Hagakure, the Book of the Samurai* (transl. William Scott Wilson), Tokyo, New York and San Francisco, 1979/1983.

Uchiyama, Koshi, Roshi, *Approach to Zen*, Japan Publications, Tokyo, 1973.

Waley, Arthur, *Three Ways of Thought in Ancient China*, Allen & Unwin, London, 1939.

Wang, Yi-T'ung, *Official Relations between China and Japan 1368–1549*, Cambridge, Mass., 1953.

Wilson, William (transl.), *Hagakure, Kondansha*, Tokyo, 1979/1983.

Watts, Alan W., *The Way of Zen*, Pantheon Books, 1957.

_____ *Nature, Man and Woman*, Pantheon Books, New York, 1958.

_____ *The Book on the Taboo Against Knowing Who You Are*, Jonathan Cape, London, 1966.

_____ 'The Art of Contemplation', in *The Alan Watts Journal*, Society for Comparative Philosophy, 1972.

_____ *Tao, The Watercourse Way*, Penguin Books, Harmondsworth, 1979.

_____ *OM, Creative Meditations*, Electronic University, USA, Celestial Arts, Millbrae, 1980.

Yanagi, Soetsu, *The Unknown Craftsman*, Kodansha, Tokyo, 1972.

Yoichi, Hirose, *Yo-sha-roku*, Japan (Tokyo?) 1675.

NOTES

PART I: HISTORICAL FOUNDATIONS

The Historical Significance of the Bow

1. Heinz, Meyer, *Geschichte der Reiterkrieger*, Stuttgart, Berlin, Cologne and Mainz 1982. A very thorough cultural and sociological investigation, which also stresses the importance of the bow for early armies of horsemen.

The History of the Bow in Japan

1. Cf. Roger Bersihand, *Histoire du Japon des origines à nos jours*, Payot, Paris, 1959.
2. John Whitney Hall wrote as late as 1954 in his *Japanese History, Guide to Japanese Reference and Research Materials* (Greenwood Press, London): 'They [the Jōmon people] had developed a composite bow, similar to the typical Japanese bow . . .'. Firstly, the composite bow is in no way typically Japanese since it existed in considerably older cultures. And secondly, that assertion, which Hall does not back with any concrete evidence, must now be viewed as mistaken in the light of more recent archaeological findings. Hoff also wrongly describes the first depiction of a Yayoi period bow (on a bronze bell) as a composite bow (cf. F. F. Hoff, Kyūdō, Berlin, 1980 – a very useful book for exclusively practical training).
3. For the social implications of the Iemoto system see Karl-Heinz Ludwig's 'Japan; Satori und Business' in: *Merkur*, No. 392, Jan. 1981.

PART II: THE SPIRITUAL FOUNDATIONS OF KYŪDŌ

Breath and Breathing

1. Almost all of today's publications on Yoga, Taoism, and Zen view breath and breathing as fulfilling a crucial function. More recent books providing an excellent account of such practical aspects of meditation include:

   Sekida Katsuki, *Zen Training – Methods and Philosophy*, New York and Tokyo, 1975.
   André van Lysebeth, *Pranayama: Yoga of Breathing*, Mandala Books, Allen & Unwin, London.
   Chang Chung-yuan, *Creativity and Taoism, A Study of Chinese Philosophy, Art and Poetry*, Harper & Row, 1970.
   Taisen Deshimaru-Rōshi, *The Zen Way to the Martial Arts*, Rider, London, 1983.
   Yogi Ramacharaka, *Hatha Yoga or the Yogi Philosophy of Physical Well-*

Being, L. N. Fowler, London.

Yogacharya Ramesh Chander, *Tantric Yoga – Techniques and Rituals for Health, Wealth, Success*, New Delhi.

2. Alan Watts, *The Art of Contemplation*, Pantheon, 1973 (translated from the German edition: Watts/Lama Anagavika Govinda, *Die Kunst der Kontemplation*, Freiburg/Br, 2nd ed, 1979, p. 7).

3. John Blofeld, *The Secret and Sublime, Taoist Mysteries and Magic*, George Allen & Unwin, London, 1973, pp. 121ff. The fact that early Taoists utilised archery as a means of meditation is exemplified in the philosopher Lieh-tzu, who was an enthusiastic bowman, referring to archery in several chapters of his work. See *The Book of Lieh-tzu* translated by A. C. Graham, London, 1960.

4. Johann Wolfgang von Goethe, *Selected Poems*, trans. by Christopher Middleton, John Calder, London, 1983, p. 207.
   The original German runs:
   > Und so lang du das nicht hast,
   > Dieses Stirb und Werde.
   > Bist du nur ein trüber Gast
   > Auf der dunklen Erde.

5. Cf. Lao-Tzu, *Tao Te Ching*, a new translation by Gia-Fu Feng and Jane English, Wildwood House, London, 1972.

6. See J. J. M. de Groot, *Religion in China. Universism: A Key to the Study of Taoism and Confucianism*, C. P. Putnam's Sons, New York and London, 1912. In my opinion de Groot's work still provides one of the most thorough treatments of the Tao of man, the Tao of the universe, and the relationship between the two, apart from examining all aspects of Taoism and Confucianism.

7. *Tao Te Ching*, chapter 63.

8. See the excellent *Creativity and Taoism*, op. cit. pp. 135ff.

9. *Tao Te Ching*, op. cit., chapter 16.

10. *Tao Te Ching*, op. cit., chapter 10.

11. de Groot, *Religion in China*, op. cit., p. 156.

12. Cf. Blofeld, *The Secret and Sublime*, op. cit., p. 134: 'The spirit of the valley is undying; it is called the mysterious female, whose portal is known as the fundament of heaven and earth. Though [its essence] if preserved is delicate, use cannot exhaust it'.

13. *Chuang Tzu, Taoist Philosopher and Chinese Mystic*, translated from the Chinese by Herbert A. Giles, George Allen & Unwin, London 1961, chapter 6.

14. Ibid, chapter 15.

15. These spiritual centres, or centres of psycho-physical cosmic subtle energy, are today usually called *chakras* after Tantra. The channels linking the individual chakras are known as *nadis*.

16. Cf. Sekida Katsuki, *Zen Training – Methods and Philosophy*, op. cit., particularly the chapters on 'Breathing in Zazen' and 'The Tanden'.

The Way and the Ways

1. *Tao Te Ching*, op. cit., chapter 1.
2. de Groot, *Religion in China*, op. cit., p. 6.

3. For a survey of the development and utilisation of the term 'Way' in Japanese culture, see Horst Hammitzsch, 'Zum Begriff "Weg" im Rahmen der japanischen Künste', in *Nachrichten der OAG*, No. 82, 1957.
4. Cf. H. Munsterberg's comprehensive *Zen-Kunst*, Cologne, 1978.
5. Blofeld, *The Secret and Sublime*, op. cit., pp. 121ff.

Tao, Zen, and Archery

1. Quoted from Sukie Colgrave, *The Spirit of the Valley, Androgyny and Chinese Thought*, Virago, London, 1979, p. 56.
2. *Tao Te Ching*, op. cit., chapter 11.
3. Ibid., chapter 12.
4. D. T. Suzuki, *An Introduction to Zen Buddhism*, Arrow Books, London, 1959, pp. 46ff.
5. Ibid., pp. 50ff.
6. See Hans Paeschke, 'Zen' in *Merkur*, June 1959, p. 504.
7. Suzuki, *An Introduction to Zen Buddhism*, op. cit., pp. 51ff.
8. D. T. Suzuki, *Zen and Japanese Culture*, Princeton University Press, New York, 1970, p. 120.
9. See Horst Tiwald, *Psycho-Training im Kampf- und Budo-Sport*, Ahrensburg, 1981.
10. Cf. D. T. Suzuki, *Mysticism: Christian and Buddhist*, George Allen & Unwin, London, 1957, pp. 129ff.
11. *Chuang Tzu, Taoist Philosopher and Chinese Mystic*, op. cit., Book II, p. 42.
12. Lama Anagarika Govinda, Preface to: *Meditations-Sutras des Mahayana-Buddhismus*, Vol. II, Zürich 1956 – quoted in Kurt Brasch, *Zenga – Zen-Malerei*, Tokyo, 1961, p. 2.
13. Blofeld, *The Secret and Sublime*, op. cit., p. 130.
14. See *Pi yen lu: The Blue Cliff Record*, translated by Thomas and J. C. Cleary, Shambhala, Boulder and London, 1977.
15. Cf. Colegrave, *The Spirit of the Valley*, p. 191: 'The search for the Self is the search for the microcosm of the universe, the image of the Dao in which all is reflected. It is not a search which demands that we become more than we are by nature, but a search in which we learn to acknowledge that we are more than we know'.
16. Chuang Tzu, op. cit., Book XVIII, pp. 173ff.

Bushidō – The Way of the Warrior

1. Cf. Tiwald, *Psycho-Training im Kampf- und Budo-Sport*, op. cit., pp. 70ff. Tiwald's objective is to re-establish the spiritual aspect of European sport *vis-à-vis* physical and technical emphases. His approach is based on Taoism and Zen, successfully deploying their spiritual foundations for the enrichment of Western sport. A trail-blazing work for the future of Western sport.
2. Hans Paeschke, 'Zen', in *Merkur*, June 1959, p. 516.
3. See Robert Schinzinger, 'Das Bild des Menschen in der japanischen Tradition der Vorkriegsphilosophie' in: *Neue Anthropologie*, Vol. 6 – Philosophische Anthropologie, p. 195.
4. Suzuki, *Zen and Japanese Culture*, op. cit., p. 63.
5. *Tao Te Ching*, op. cit., chapter 31.

6. Ibid., chapter 22.
7. Suzuki, *Zen and Japanese Culture*, op. cit., p. 65.
8. Ibid., p. 78.
9. The *Hagakure* (literally 'Hidden Under The Leaves') is a collection of episodes, anecdotes, aphorisms, etc., relating to Bushidō. Zen monks played a part in its compilation. The complete two-volume Japanese text was published in Tokyo in 1937. A selection in English translation is contained in : *Hagakure, the Book of the Samurai*, Yamamoto Tsunetomo, trans. William Scott Wilson, Tokyo, New York and San Francisco 1979/1983.
10. *The Book of Lieh-Tzu*, op. cit., p. 113.
11. *Tao Te Ching*, op. cit., chapter 69.
12. Taisen Deshimaru-Rōshi, *La Pratique du Zen*, Edition Seghers, Paris, 1977.

Kyūdō and Ceremony

1. Cf. Robert Schinzinger, *Japanisches Denken*, Berlin, 1983, p. 30.
2. *The Sayings of Confucius*, translated by Leonard A. Lyall, Longmans Green and Co., New York, Bombay and Calcutta, 1909 (VI, 16), p. 27.
3. Ibid., (XV, 32), p. 86.
4. Confucius, *The Analects*, translated by D. C. Lau, Penguin Classics, Harmondsworth (I, 12) p. 61.
5. Ibid. (III, 7), p. 68.
6. Cf. Werner Rilz, 'Konfuzianismus und Japan', manuscript, Kobe, 1983.

Spirit and Technique

1. Eugen Herrigel, *Zen in the Art of Archery*, Arkana, London, Melbourne, and Henley 1985.
2. Ibid., chapter II, pp. 25–9.
3. On 'active reflection' see Robert Schinzinger, *Japanisches Denken*, op. cit., pp. 57–75, where the author provides a condensed summary of Nishida's philosophy.
4. Herrigel, *Zen in the Art of Archery*, op. cit., p. 18.
5. See Taisen Deshimaru-Rōshi, *The Zen Way to the Martial Arts*, op. cit., pp. 37ff:

   'People who do not want to follow the teaching of Zen, the true foundation of Bushidō, do not have to do so. They're simply using the martial arts as playthings; to them they are sports like any others.

   'But people who want to lead their lives on a higher dimension do have to understand.

   'Nobody can be compelled and nobody can be criticised. The first lot are like children playing with toy cars, while the second drive real automobiles. I have nothing against sports; they train the body and develop stamina and endurance. But the spirit of competition and power that presides over them is not good; it reflects a distorted vision of life. The root of the martial arts is not there.

   'The teachers are partly responsible for this state of affairs; they train the body and teach technique, but do nothing for consciousness. As a result their pupils fight to win, like children playing war games. There is no wisdom in this approach and it is no use at all in the business of managing one's life.

'What good to them is their technique in everyday life?

'Sports are only amusement and in the end, because of the spirit of competition, they wear out the body. That is why the martial arts should strive to recapture their original dimension. In the spirit of Zen and Budō everyday life becomes the contest. There must be awareness at every moment – getting up in the morning, working, eating, going to bed. That is the place for mastery of the self.'

6. That is particularly stressed by Karl Gauhofer and Margarete Streicher. See *Natürliches Turnen*, 5 vols., 1949.
7. Tiwald correctly emphasises that point: *Psycho-Training im Kampf- und Budo-Sport*, op. cit.
8. *The Book of Lieh-tzu*, op. cit., Chapter IV, 2, pp. 77f.
9. Ibid., Chapter 11, 5, pp. 38f.
10. Such 'demonstrations of skill' as performed here by Lieh-tzu should not be dismissed out of hand. Such marvels are, however, superficialities, not the objective of training – as Lieh-tzu makes clear with his cup of water. We should always regard such astonishing manifestations – to which Herrigel unfortunately attached considerable importance – as what they are intended to be : a game and by-product of the Way. I have seen such feats with my own eyes, but then the same master also went on to shoot badly. Both occasioned a smile; neither is a yardstick for the level the archer has achieved on his Way.

PART III: THE PRACTICE OF KYŪDŌ

Preparations

1. Tiwald, *Psycho-Training im Kampf- und Budo-Sport*, op. cit., pp. 54ff. The situation facing German Jūdō was also described in *Deutsches Judo-Magazin*, April 1983, pp. 32ff, where training based on 'drilling' isolated individual movements and techniques is seen as the reason for a growing lack of interest in this sport. Thousands are leaving the German Jūdō Association at a time when there is a great boom in the other Budō sports.

Hassetsu – The Eight Stages leading to Release of the Arrow and Stepping Back from the Shooting Line

1. *Chuang Tzu, Taoist Philosopher and Chinese Mystic*, op. cit., p. 212.

Eastern Practices for Westerners?

1. That prejudice is particularly convincingly refuted in Robert Schinzinger, *Nachahmung und Eigenständigkeit in der japanischen Kultur*, Druck Lesestube, Kobe and Japan, 1979.
2. Karl Löwith, *Unterschied von Ost und West*, Sanshusha-Verlag, Tokyo, 1972, p. 8.
3. Ibid., p. 9.
4. Ibid., p. 11.
5. D. T. Suzuki wrote his otherwise excellent works as a scholar and philosopher, and for that reason they can make only a very limited

contribution to practical aspects of the Way.
6. Sen Soshitsu, 'Chadō – The Way of Tea and its Relevance to Modern Life' in *Mainichi Daily News*, 10.1.1982. See also Soshitsu's 'Chanoyu – a Quest for Peacefulness' in *Mainichi Daily News*, a series of twenty articles from March to July 1983.
7. Alan Watts (1915–1974) knew both Eastern and Western ways of thinking, and his works (See Bibliography) are one of the most convincing syntheses yet achieved between 'East' and 'West'.

PART IV: THE KYŪDŌ ARCHER'S EQUIPMENT

The Modern Kyūdō Bow

1. The best account I know of the essential nature of symmetry and asymmetry in Taoism and Zen is Erwin Reisner, 'Sukiya – die Symbolsprache des japanischen Teeraums', in *Merkur*, No. 132, 1959, pp. 111–24.
2. Ibid., p. 114.
3. Hirose Yoichi, *Yo-sha-roku*, Japan (Tokyo?), 1675.